THE WORLD WAR 2 TRIVIA BOOK

Interesting Stories and Random
Facts from the Second World War

BY
**DWAYNE WALKER
& BILL O'NEILL**

DON'T FORGET YOUR FREE BOOKS

GET THEM FOR FREE ON
WWW.TRIVIABILL.COM

CONTENTS

INTRODUCTION

What do you know about World War Two?

You know the big events: the Nazis, Pearl Harbour, the Holocaust, Hiroshima. I bet you know the major players: The Allied powers (Britain, France, the United States, and the Soviet Union, plus others) and the Axis powers (Germany, Japan, and Italy, plus others). You definitely know Adolf Hitler, and you've probably heard of Winston Churchill, Joseph Stalin, Franklin Delano Roosevelt, Benito Mussolini, and Emperor Hirohito.

But have you ever wondered who started World War Two? What really happened in Hitler's "Third Reich"? Why does France have a reputation for surrendering? Why shouldn't you invade Russia in the winter?

If you've ever been curious about the answers to those questions or hundreds of others about the biggest war in history, then this is the book for you. It's full of stories that will make history come alive.

This isn't your ordinary history book. It will guide

you through the main events and battles of World War Two, but it's not just a timeline of battles, deaths, and old men in suits making decisions about politics! This book will teach you all the nitty-gritty details and weird facts that made World War Two such a strange, fascinating war. By the time you're done this book, you're going to be an expert—and not just in the parts of the war that your history teacher wanted you to know about.

World War Two itself only lasted for six years (although some people would argue it lasted fourteen —and you're going to find out why!), but we're going to cover almost a century of history here. We'll go all the way back to 1918 to explain why Germany was in such bad shape that they allowed Adolf Hitler to become dictator. We'll also go all the way forward to 2017 to see why Christopher Nolan made four hundred billion dollars with a movie about one little battle.

While this book is mostly chronological, meaning it starts at the beginning of World War Two and ends at the end, we're going to jump around while we talk about the opening of the war, the countries that played the biggest roles, the end of the war, and then some fun facts about how World War Two affected culture—especially the world of film, which was a new, exciting kind of media during World War Two!

It's broken up into six easy chapters, each with fifteen

stories about the chapter's main topic. They'll introduce you to colourful characters, from "Mad Jack" Churchill to Unity Mitford. They'll also help you understand the hard facts and the politics well enough to discuss them at your next dinner party or history class. Each chapter also comes with a whole section full of quick, surprising facts to wow your friends and a few challenging trivia questions to test your knowledge!

Some of the facts you're about to learn are sad. Some are scary. Some are sexy. And some are downright strange!

So get ready to find out…

Which British soldier shot Germans with a bow and arrow?

Why was the United States going to stay out of the war?

How did the Canadians steal airplanes for the British?

What does an orange soft drink have to do with Hitler?

And much, much more!

CHAPTER ONE

THE START OF THE WAR

World War Two began in 1939, when Britain and France declared war on Germany. However, the story goes back much further than that, with drama, lies, and political intrigue. You probably know that Britain and France declared war because of Nazi war crimes, but you might not know what led up to that, why war wasn't declared sooner, or even what those war crimes technically were. Read on to learn some interesting facts about events that led to the deadliest war in human history.

The Invasion of Manchuria

If we're talking about World War Two from a chronological standpoint, it makes sense to start not in Nazi Germany but in Japan.

World War Two actually started as two different wars that merged together over time. The war in Europe had Britain, France, and the Soviet Union (as well as their colonial properties like Canada and Australia) on one side and Germany and Italy on the other. But there was another war that started a little earlier—in 1937, or maybe even as early as 1931—and that was the war in the Pacific. This war had Japan on one side and on the other side mainland China and eventually the United States.

On September 18, 1931, the Empire of Japan invaded Manchuria (a province on the border of China and Russia) and shocked the western world with their violent war tactics. The League of Nations (the proto-UN developed after World War One to try to stop another war from happening) tried to order Japan to stop the invasion, but Japan blatantly ignored them. It turned out that the League of Nations was completely powerless in the face of any nation that decided to flaunt their rules. The only consequence the League of Nations could exact was to remove Japan from the League, which wasn't much of a consequence at all since Japan didn't want to be in it anyway.

While this was going on, other world leaders were taking notes. Adolf Hitler was quick to notice how powerless the League of Nations was against another country's aggressive action. It wasn't long until he took Japan's lead and invaded his own neighbours without fear of retribution.

The Second Sino-Japanese War

Japan moved on from Manchuria to the rest of China in 1937, in what was called the Second Sino-Japanese War. Japan's success in invading Manchuria and establishing a puppet state gave them the confidence to move towards some of China's bigger ports, like Beijing. The invasion that marks the start of the Second Sino-Japanese War happened when the Japanese crossed the Marco Polo Bridge into Beijing, quickly capturing the biggest cities of mainland China.

The Japanese army soon reached Nanking, which was the capital of China at the time. For six weeks, they looted, raped, and killed Chinese civilians. Japanese military records were destroyed immediately after the war, but estimates range from 40,000 dead to over 300,000 dead.

The 1937 census claimed that the population of Nanking was just over one million people. However, when it became clear that Japan was planning on invading, hundreds of thousands of citizens fled the city. The number of civilians left in Nanking at the time of the massacre was not documented, but it's estimated to be between 200,000 and 500,000 (not counting soldiers). This means that anywhere from one tenth of the people left to virtually 100% of the city could have been wiped out. The real fraction was probably around one third or one quarter of everyone left in Nanking killed, not to mention the numbers of rapes and non-deadly injuries.

The Stand at Shanghai

China quickly realized that they didn't have the resources or the military experience to fight off the Japanese army successfully. However, they also knew that they wouldn't get any outside help if they just surrendered. They also knew that the political differences between the Chinese Nationalist Party and the Communist Party of China were making them an easy target, since they were so focussed on fighting each other that they couldn't build a force against Japan.

Chiang Kai-shek, the Chairman of the National Military Council of China, knew that he had to do something to fight off the Japanese army while also boosting his people's morale. So, he organized the Battle of Shanghai, a three-and-a-half-month battle at China's biggest, most industrial city.

The soldiers that Chiang sent to the Battle of Shanghai had been trained in Germany (remember, this was before Japan and Germany got on the same side of the war). Although their weapons were small-scale and their troops were much less prepared, they shocked the world with how long they held out. Their mere presence shook the Japanese morale, since they had become so convinced of their own superiority.

Unfortunately for China, most of their best soldiers were killed in the battle, and they didn't garner the foreign support they were hoping for. Europe was a little preoccupied with their own increasingly powerful, unchecked, nationalist government...

Flashback: The Treaty of Versailles

Japan wasn't the only nation that was getting interested in taking over bits of other countries. This ideology, which is called *expansionism*, turns up in cultures from Ancient Rome to the American West, but in twentieth century Europe, one particular country was interested in expanding: Germany.

Let's take a step back in time. After World War One, Germany was essentially forced to accept responsibility for the war and to give up its territories (and pay the equivalent of four and a half billion modern American dollars in reparations) to the winning side. This was written in a clause called the "War Guilt Clause" in the Treaty of Versailles, the treaty that laid out the terms for peace after World War One.

World War One wasn't really Germany's fault. A hundred years of simmering tensions and entangling alliances (combined with some unexpected leaps in technology that sent the death count soaring) were to blame. Germany could reasonably shoulder some responsibility, but so could Britain, France, and every other country involved. But, as is always the case for wars, the winners got to decide what to do with the losers, and the winning powers (especially France) wanted to weaken Germany as much as possible, hence the extreme punishment.

Even at the time, people all over the world were saying that this was a bad idea. The world-famous economist John Maynard Keynes said that this was too harsh and pointed out that there was no way Germany could afford the reparations without sending the country into economic disaster.

There were also some people who said it was too lenient on Germany, and while there's no way that the terms could be described as "lenient" in hindsight, they may have had a point in a way. The harsher punishment, a full-on military occupation of Germany, would have weakened the country enough to stop it from rebelling. As it was, the Treaty of Versailles hit an awkward middle ground—way too harsh for Germany to manage but not harsh enough to squash the inevitable backlash.

It's really important to understand this if you want to understand why the Nazis rose to power in Germany. It wasn't just that everyone turned evil at the same time. The country got put in a dire situation, and some power-hungry politicians saw an opportunity to turn righteous anger into hate and nationalism.

Lebensraum

The word *Lebensraum* was first used in 1860, more than half a century before Nazism even began to take shape. *Lebensraum* literally means "living space" in German, and it wasn't until 1901 that the essay "*Lebensraum*" was written by Friedrich Ratzel to describe how physical geography shapes society. He argued that geographical factors shape the focusses that a society has, and that a strong society should, theoretically, expand organically through space over time, rather than being constrained by artificial political boundaries.

Ratzel did suggest in his book and essay on the subject that because Germany was a strong state (remember, 1901 was just before World War One), Germany should be able to expand into spaces that were controlled by weaker states.

This idea became very popular in German thought over the next decade, but it really took off after the Treaty of Versailles for two reasons. First, Germany was forced to hand over all their territories to the winners of the war, and second, the massive reparations it was forced to pay caused an overwhelming food shortage. Both of these factors made Germany eager to expand and to take back the *Lebensraum* that many Germans felt was rightfully theirs.

Lebensraum was a major concept that Adolf Hitler discussed in his autobiography *Mein Kampf*. He claimed that Germany's natural superiority meant that it rightfully *should* own the territory of Eastern Europe, and that any attempts to constrain it were artificial and destined to fail. Germany's economic distress, according to this interpretation, was being caused by attempted constraints being put on Germany's *Lebensraum*.

This idea was hugely appealing to the German people of the time, who were suffering from crippling economic depression under the post-Treaty of Versailles regime. The idea of *Lebensraum* offered an explanation for their suffering, as well as appealing to a sense of pride by claiming that their culture and race was naturally superior to the cultures and races of the people into whose territory they would expand. It didn't take long after the publication of *Mein Kampf* in 1925 for Hitler and his *Lebensraum*-focussed ideology to rise to power.

Adolf Hitler: Artist?

Adolf Hitler, the *Führer* (literally "guide," the political leader) of Germany, didn't start out as a politician. If you'd told eighteen-year-old Adolf that he was going to become the most notorious dictator in world history, he'd probably have laughed in your face, because when he was eighteen, in 1907, he was trying (and failing) to get into art school!

Hitler applied to the Academy of Fine Arts Vienna in 1907 (and again, next year, in 1908) because he had ambitions of becoming a professional artist. He was very skilled at painting architecture and liked to paint landscapes featuring the Greek and Roman-influenced buildings of Italy and Austria-Hungary.

Hitler claimed to like Renaissance art, since it was technically powerful and the symbolism was clear. We can guess he probably wasn't a big fan of the expressionists and modernists that were getting more attention in the early twentieth century for their crazy, abstract paintings. The Great German Art Exhibit that he set up refused to allow any expressionist, Dadaist, or cubist art styles, as well as any art that depicted weakness or racial impurity.

Unfortunately for the western world, Hitler got rejected from art school both times he applied. He worked for a while painting postcards in Vienna before joining the army in World War One, and never made much of a career of it.

Hitler's Image

Through the lens of hindsight, it seems crazy that anyone could gain so much power by standing on a pulpit and screaming about the evils of the Jews. But Hitler and his team actually went to a lot of trouble to make him seem like an attractive leader. There was a lot of propaganda about how evil his enemies were, but there were also a lot of details that went into making Hitler himself a striking, memorable, and appealing figure.

For one thing, he was not like the old leaders. German leaders in World War One were rich, old-fashioned, and had huge moustaches. Hitler came from a modest background, was focussed on the future rather than the past, and sported a stylish postage-stamp moustache that has become iconic.

Mentioning Hitler's moustache might seem like a trivial detail, but it was all part of his "look." More than any other leader of the modern world, Hitler created a distinctly stylish "image" for himself and his army. He sported the newest fashion in facial hair, he was always surrounded by adoring crowds of beautiful people, and he even had fashion designer Hugo Boss design the sleek black SS uniforms to be both intimidating and appealing. Everything about Hitler's image made him look like the man that every German citizen wanted to be.

Man of the Year

In 1938, just one year before Germany and Britain went to war, Adolf Hitler was named "Man of the Year" by *Time Magazine*. The article profiling him, which is available online, isn't exactly favourable towards him, but it does seem to compliment his bravery and political energy. "He had torn the treaty of Versailles to shreds... before the eyes of a horrified and apparently impotent world," the article reads.

Some people are shocked to hear that such an obviously dangerous man could be immortalized as "Man of the Year" (and other people wryly bring this up when their least favourite politician appears on *Time's* cover), but the "Man of the Year" award goes to the most influential person of the year, not the "best." And Hitler was certainly influential!

The article describes Hitler's shockingly effective political strategies with a tone of shock and awe. "All these events were shocking to nations which had defeated Germany on the battlefield only 20 years before," it says when describing how Hitler gained military power all over Europe. "[When he] won a free hand for himself in Eastern Europe by getting a "hands-off" promise from powerful Britain (and later France), Adolf Hitler without a doubt became 1938's Man of the Year."

Of course, remember that *Time Magazine* is an American publication. With the buffer of the Atlantic Ocean between them and the Nazis, the United States might have been just a *little* more complimentary towards Hitler than his neighbours might have been if they were in charge of naming "Man of the Year."

Appeasement

Speaking of Hitler's neighbours, things were getting pretty tense between Germany and Britain. Hitler was becoming braver and braver in his military activities—and it's hard to be surprised by that, because the British had adopted a policy called "appeasement" to Germany (and its partner in fascism, Italy).

Appeasement was a policy put in place by Neville Chamberlain, the British Prime Minister, to try to avert war. His theory was that trying to prevent Germany from getting what it wanted would cause more harm than good in the long run. Therefore, Britain's official foreign policy would be that they would fulfill Germany's wishes, "provided they appeared legitimate and were not enforced with violence," (described in German newspaper *Der Spiegel*). Chamberlain was aware that the British Empire's resources were limited and that they didn't really have the power to stop Hitler, so cooperating with him seemed like the better option.

However, as anyone who's dealt with a spoiled child will know, giving them what they want doesn't solve the problem. Hitler demanded the right to expand Germany into the neighbouring *Sudetenland*, violating the non-military policies in the Treaty of Versailles. When Hitler saw that he could do that without punishment, it was just a small step to expanding into Czechoslovakia and Poland.

The appeasement policy came from a genuine attempt to prevent another mass slaughter like the one that Europe had suffered in World War One. However, when Chamberlain let Hitler get away with breaking the terms of the Treaty, it only bolstered Hitler's confidence. Instead of becoming satisfied, he just became more confident that he could get away with anything.

The Invasion of Poland

You might think that Britain and France declared war on Germany because of the Holocaust and the massacre of Jewish civilians, but you'd be wrong. The scale of Hitler's concentration camps and mass murder of innocent Jewish people didn't come to light until much later. Britain and France declared war on Germany because Hitler invaded Poland, which went against the deal that Hitler had made with other European leaders.

Hitler had already seen that Britain was unwilling to enforce the terms of the Treaty of Versailles. Neville Chamberlain was practicing a policy of appeasement, allowing Hitler to build a military power even though he was technically not allowed to.

It was already pretty clear to the Nazis that no one wanted to be the ones to stand up and oppose them.

This became even more obvious in the 1930s, as Japan started doing what Germany was only considering.

In 1931, Japan invaded Manchuria with no consequences from the international government. Throughout the 1930s, foreign powers looked away as the Japanese army marched through China, leaving a trail of corpses in their wake. In 1937, when China took a stand against the Japanese army at the Battle of Shanghai, not a single foreign power came to their aid.

The lesson Hitler took from this was clear: no one wanted to get into a war, so no one wanted to take any action against an aggressive nation. He had an unblocked path to power.

America Tries to Remain Neutral

So far, you've learned about what was happening in East Asia (the war between China and Japan) and in West Europe (Germany's aggressive policies towards its neighbours). But there's one major player that we haven't talked about much... the United States.

The United States didn't officially enter World War Two until 1941, two years after Britain, France, Germany, and Italy declared war on each other. We'll talk later about the United States' reasons for entering the war when they did, but they weren't exactly ignoring what was happening in the lead-up.

In World War One, the United States held off, and

entered the war much later than the other players did. This meant that it hadn't been nearly as devastated by its effects as other countries, but no one could claim that it had been a fun time. Like most countries, the US was reluctant to get into another war.

In the 1920s, America signed a lot of disarmament and non-aggression pacts, like 1928's Kellogg-Briand Pact, pledging not to go to war with any of the other people who signed it. The other signers included Germany, Poland, Africa, Japan, Britain, and France, and later expanded to include Serbia, China, Hungary, and the Soviet Union, so you can see how well that pact turned out.

In the 1930s, it became clear that no one was planning to honour the pact. It didn't stop Japan from invading Manchuria, or Germany from developing a high-powered new army. So the United States started passing the Neutrality Acts instead, which banned them from loaning money or selling weapons to any country at war. Congress believed this would keep States out of Europe's business.

However, when war broke out, most Americans (including the president, Franklin Delano Roosevelt) sympathized pretty strongly with the British. It was obvious that Germany was the aggressor, and although there were plenty of people who disagreed, the general attitude in America was that they should be doing *something* to help the Allies (especially Britain).

American Planes

The American Air Force found one way to help Britain without violating any of their neutrality agreements... supplying them with planes. The British Air Force desperately needed planes for their military, and the US had lots of planes but couldn't sell them to the British because that would count as selling weapons to a country at war.

So the States enlisted the help of their neighbours – Britain's colony, Canada. American pilots flew their planes to the border between Canada and the United States (which was mostly farmland), and landed them in the fields... and left them there. Then, overnight, Canadian pilots would cross down into the States, and tow the planes north, into Canadian lands.

Since there was no fence, wall, or other visual delineation between Canada and the US, Canadians could claim that they thought the planes were in Canadian territory... while Americans could claim that they just *happened* to leave their planes overnight, and had no way of knowing they would be stolen!

The Soviet Union Enters the War

On August 23ʳᵈ, 1939, just one week before Hitler invaded Poland, the Soviet Union signed a pact with the Nazis, agreeing not to go to war with them. There was even some talk of the Soviet Union becoming an

Axis power, one of Hitler's official allies. Stalin, the leader of the Soviet Union, even supported Hitler's plan to invade Poland.

There was a lot of suspicion between these two nations, which grew greater over time. The Soviet Union started to suspect that Germany planned to invade them as soon as they had conquered Britain. Stalin tried to demonstrate his nation's positive feelings towards Germany by agreeing not to fight against Japan in East Asia, but that wasn't enough to prevent tensions between them.

It's frankly surprising that the Soviet Union ever thought they could have peaceful diplomatic relations with Germany, since communists were one of Hitler's many targets, and the Soviet Union was a communist nation.

This pact didn't last long – in the summer of 1941, Hitler invaded Soviet territories along their shared border.

Historian and former military intelligence officer Viktor Suvorov claimed that Stalin was planning to invade Germany around the same time, and Hitler simply made the move first. Either way, it wasn't long before the Soviet Union had decided its goals were more in line with the Allies than the Axis, and launched a serious defence against German attacks.

America Enters the War

In 1939, the United States was generally sympathetic to the Allied powers, and were willing to bend the rules of their non-aggression pacts a bit to help them out, but they had no plans to actually enter the war. But everything changed in 1941 with the Japanese bombing of Pearl Harbour.

Pearl Harbour was the home of a major US military base in Hawaii, which is located right in the middle of the Pacific Ocean between the United States and Japan. It was the natural place for Japan to attack as they expanded into the Pacific. The attack was a surprise, for although the United States had provided some money to China to help them in their war against Japan, they were a big step away from anything resembling war. They even continued to sell oil to Japan into 1940.

In 1941, the United States decided to start building up a presence in the Pacific to try to discourage Japan from attacking, but boy did that backfire! Instead of being intimidated into backing down, Japan decided to retaliate with a pre-emptive strike against the seat of the US's Pacific power.

The day after the attack, Franklin Delano Roosevelt made a speech calling for war with Japan, and Congress took less than an hour to agree.

They weren't the only ones. This was the point when

Japan truly entered onto the playing field of World War Two. Winston Churchill, the newly elected Prime Minister of Britain, had promised that if Japan attacked the United States, Britain would declare war on Japan "within the hour."

Three days later, Germany and Italy, who had been building relations with Japan, also declared war on the United States in solidarity. This wasn't part of their official pact, but it was obvious that since Britain had declared war on the US's enemy, the US wasn't going to wait long before declaring war on Britain's enemies.

The People's Responses to War

Finally, in 1941, all the major players of World War Two were involved: Britain, France, America, and the Soviet Union on one side, and Germany, Italy, and Japan on the other.

Frankly, no one was very happy to be going into war. While the onset of World War One had been seen as glorious and patriotic, views between 1939 and 1941 were much more cynical. There was public outcry at the fact that pretty much every single country had violated at least one pact or treaty to enter the war. Young people were reluctant to enter another bloodbath like the one in 1914, and soldiers who had lived through World War One were even more fearful.

In each country, politicians, social leaders, and media creators desperately tried to bolster morale. From German films about the natural superiority of the German race like the massively anti-Semitic *The Eternal Jew* (portraying Jews as depraved, parasitic, abnormal people to Disney Studio's famous "Nazi Donald Duck" cartoon *Der Führer's Face* (lampooning the Nazi regime's overblown shows of nationalism), people who had the power to boost morale were desperate to do so in the face of a grim, deadly war that no one really wanted to enter.

RANDOM FACTS

1. Japan never *technically* declared war on China during the Sino-Japanese war. If they had, they might have faced more intervention from other countries. Because of this, for decades, it was referred to as an "incident" rather than a "war" in Japan.

2. In the Treaty of Versailles, American president Woodrow Wilson cautioned that the terms of the treaty would be accepted "in humiliation, under duress, at an intolerable sacrifice, and would leave a sting, a resentment, a bitter memory upon which terms of peace would rest, not permanently, but only as upon quicksand." However, even he couldn't have guessed how fast peace would fall apart.

3. Hitler clung on to his dream of professional art long after starting his political career. In 1939, right before the outbreak of war, he allegedly told the British ambassador, "once the Polish question is settled, I want to end my life as an artist."

4. Hitler was offered the opportunity to go to architectural school instead of art school, since that was clearly what he was most interested in drawing. However, this would have required him

to return to high school, which he did not want to do, so he turned down the opportunity.

5. Hitler painted a self-portrait when he was 21, but his portrait didn't have a face. Some art critics have taken this as a grim foreshadowing of his lack of interest in human life.

6. In his four years in the German army in World War One, Hitler never rose higher than the rank of a corporal. *Ouch*.

7. King Edward VIII of England abdicated the throne in 1936 to marry a divorcee who also happened to be an open Nazi sympathizer. There were even claims at the time that she was an agent of Hitler sent to destabilize the British throne.

8. While most Americans sympathized with Britain in World War Two, the United States did have a Nazi party called the "German American Bund" or "German American Federation," made up of German immigrants.

9. Some non-Germans in America also sympathized with the Nazis for various reasons, ranging from feeling like they were unfairly punished in the Treaty of Versailles to agreeing with their policies about Jews.

10. Henry Ford, creator and owner of Ford Motors, famously continued to do business with Nazi

Germany into World War Two. He had sponsored an openly anti-Jewish newspaper and allegedly had a picture of Hitler in his office.

11. One of the reasons that Germany was in such a terrible economic state in the 1920s was inflation, meaning that money became worth less and less. This affected the whole world (and was one of the main causes of the Great Depression), but Germany felt it especially badly. Their currency, the *mark*, dropped in value exponentially over just a few years. During World War One, one American dollar was worth about five marks. By November 1923, one American dollar was worth no less than *four trillion marks*.

12. People who opposed the United States entering World War Two were known as "isolationists," since they believed that America should be *isolated* from European events.

13. Canada, one of Britain's biggest colonies, had objected at the beginning of the First World War that they were forced to go to war as soon as Britain declared it. They had declared themselves an independent Dominion in the 1860s, and thought they should have the right to declare war themselves, and Britain agreed. So when Britain declared war on Germany on September 1, 1939, Canada waited nine whole days before declaring war as well.

14. South Africa, another property of the British commonwealth, was less eager to join the war. It was legally obligated by the Polish-British Common Defence Pact to help Britain if war was declared on Poland. However, less than fifty years before, South Africa had fought against Britain in the Boer War, struggling for independence from the British Empire. During the Boer War, Germany had supported South Africa against Britain, and since many white South Africans were of German descent, they were extremely reluctant to go to war against Germany.

15. South Africa had a pro-German organization called the *Ossewabrandwag*, which was explicitly anti-British and politically opposed South Africa entering the war on the Allied side. However, the government ultimately chose to honour their pact with Britain, and leaders of the Osswabrandwag were jailed for political sabotage during the war.

16. The Americans weren't any more excited to have the Russians on their side than the Germans had been. In 1939, the New York Times wrote about the alliance between Germany and the Soviet Union: "Germany having seized the prey, Soviet Russia will seize that part of the carcass that Germany cannot use. It will play the noble role of hyena to the German lion."

17. In spite of the general mistrust around the Soviet Union (or perhaps because of it), the death rates of Soviet soldiers were astronomical. Historian Timothy Benford claims that 80% of all men born in the Soviet Union in the year 1923 were killed by the end of World War Two.

18. In 1935, a British engineer named Robert Watson-Watt was asked whether it was possible that the Germans were developing a death ray using radio waves. No such weapon was being made, but in studying the possibility, Watt ended up creating a radar detector, one of the biggest technological advances of World War Two.

19. As World War Two began, major media producers in the United States like Disney and Warner Brothers got on board creating propaganda films. Disney's *Der Führer's Face* is the most famous, but there were no fewer than nine World War Two films made starring Donald Duck alone.

20. Over the course of World War Two, the United States defence budget was increased thirty-fold, from 1.9 billion dollars to 59.8 billion dollars between 1940 and 1945.

Test Yourself – Questions and Answers

1) Which country entered World War Two first?

   a. France
   b. The United States
   c. The Soviet Union

2) Why did America want to remain neutral?

   a. It had good diplomatic relations with Germany
   b. It didn't want to enter another violent war
   c. It was afraid of losing money in armament deals

3) When did Japan invade Manchuria?

   a. 1939
   b. 1931
   c. 1937

4) Which of these famous businesspeople *didn't* support the Nazis?

   a. Hugo Boss
   b. Henry Ford
   c. William Fox

5) Why did Time Magazine name Adolf Hitler "Man of the Year"?

   a. He was the most influential politician of the year
   b. Time Magazine was run by Nazi sympathizers
   c. "Man of the Year" is a pejorative title, not a positive one

Answers

1. a
2. b
3. b
4. c
5. a

CHAPTER TWO

BRITAIN AND FRANCE AT WAR

When Hitler invaded Poland in 1939, Britain and France were the first major powers to declare war on Germany. After all, they had been at war with Germany not even twenty-one years earlier, and old wounds were still open. There was also a certain sense of guilt, and certainly a public outcry, with thousands of citizens blaming Hitler's aggression on the Treaty of Versailles, combined with Britain's ineffectual appeasement policies. As we have seen above, these citizens had a point, and so Britain and France leapt into action.

The British Empire in World War Two

In 1939, when Britain declared war on Germany, it had political control over a full quarter of the world's population through its dozens of colonies and commonwealths, and it planned to mobilize all of them against Germany.

However, not everyone in the British Empire liked this plan. Canada held off a couple of days before joining the war (just to prove that it could), but South Africa saw a passionate rebellion against the idea that they should go to war, and the Irish Free State, which had been a British dominion until just two years earlier (in 1937), remained neutral throughout the whole war.

Many of the countries that made up the British Empire were in the process of rebelling against the British colonial overlords. India would declare independence just a few years after the war ended. However, for the time being, most of them did end up entering the war, with varying degrees of enthusiasm.

The British Union of Fascists and National Socialists

At home, not everyone in the UK opposed the Nazis. In fact, some of them outright supported them. The British Union of Fascists and National Socialists was formed in 1932 by Oswald Mosley, and remained active until 1940, when the British government banned it.

At first, the British Union of Fascists and National Socialists (or BUF, as it was called for short), was a far-right but generally non-violent party. It supported

British isolationism, the idea that Britain should not be involved in European events – which was a popular view after the carnage of World War One!

However, as the decade progressed, Hitler's anti-Semitism was becoming more and more prominent, and the BUF responded by increasing their own focus on racist rhetoric. This turned a lot of people off – especially when the BUF showed that they were willing to use violence against the people they didn't like.

The death knell for the BUF's popularity was the Battle of Cable Street in 1936, when violence broke out at a BUF demonstration. The BUF marched through a Jewish neighbourhood in London, loudly proclaiming their anti-Jewish rhetoric. Some 20,000 anti-fascist demonstrators staged a counter-protest, and things got ugly quickly, as members of both parties fought with improvised weapons, and the London police force cracked down violently on the anti-fascism protesters.

The resistance that the BUF faced made it clear that the general public did not support British fascism, but the BUF didn't disband until they were forcibly shut down by the British government, and their leader, Oswald Mosley, was imprisoned for the duration of the war.

Unity Mitford

If you want a figure from British World War Two history who seems to have stepped straight out of a soap opera, Unity Mitford is your woman. The sister of Oswald Mosley's wife, Unity became infamous in Britain for her support of the Nazi party—and her alleged affair with Adolf Hitler.

In the 1930s, Unity was only one of the many Brits who fraternized with the Nazis in Germany. She wrote dozens of letters to the British press in support of Hitler and the Nazis. She even wrote an open letter to one German paper, saying "We think with joy of the day when we will be able to say England for the English! Out with the Jews! Please publish my name in full, I want everyone to know I am a Jew Hater."

According to Albert Speer's memoir of his time inside the Nazi party, Unity even personally begged Hitler to make a deal with Britain so that their countries wouldn't go to war. Her close personal relationship with Hitler certainly got people talking, both in Britain and in Germany.

Unity was in Munich, Germany, when war finally broke out between Britain and Germany. She was so distraught that she took a pistol (that Hitler had given her) and shot herself in the head. However, clearly it wasn't a very good pistol, and she survived and was hospitalized. Hitler paid her bills, frequently visited her, and even arranged for her trip back home. This has been enough for dozens of modern biographers, and Unity has been the subject of four different biographies and at least one documentary since her death.

Why Did Britain Go to War?

After the First World War, Britain was much more prepared than France to "let sleeping dogs lie" and simply "forgive" Germany for their involvement in the war (bearing in mind that there wasn't really anything to forgive at this point, since World War One was not Germany's fault). So why was Britain one of the first two countries to declare war on Germany?

Britain had been in charge of much of the discussion of appeasement that occurred in the 1930s. If Hitler broke the terms of appeasement (that is, if he invaded any lands that he'd promised not to), Britain would be held publically responsible.

On September 3, 1939, it became clear that Hitler was absolutely breaking the terms of appeasement by invading Poland and had no intentions of stopping his attack. The British Prime Minister, Neville Chamberlain, responded with an announcement on the radio:

"This morning, the British Ambassador in Berlin

handed the German Government a final note stating that, unless we heard from them by eleven o'clock that they were prepared at once to withdraw their troops from Poland, a state of war would exist between us. I have to tell you that no such understanding has been received, and that, consequently, this country is at war with Germany."

The Royal Air Force

One of Britain's biggest contributions to World War Two was the introduction of its band of fighter pilots, the Royal Air Force, or RAF. World War Two was the first war where airplanes played a major fighting role throughout the entire war. In World War One, most aircraft were used for reconnaissance, and only towards the end did air battles become a significant piece of the picture.

The Royal Air Force was formed in 1918, and is the world's oldest air force that wasn't a part of the Army or Navy. In World War Two, the RAF became one of the most crucial parts of the British military, as the Germans were pioneers of aerial warfare. The RAF flew along with Polish, Czechoslovakian, and other allied air forces. However, even combined, there were far fewer of them than there were German airplanes.

The small numbers in the RAF made it all the more impressive when they did manage to ward off Hitler's attacks. The most famous conflict was the Battle of

Britain in 1940. This campaign went on for almost four months and then bled into the Blitz, the famous German night attacks on England.

The German aim in the Battle of Britain was to bully Britain into a peace settlement by attacking their infrastructure (and later, their citizens). The Germans thought that attacking Britain by air would be easier than doing it by sea, since Britain had historically controlled the ocean with the Royal Navy.

But the Germans were wrong. Even though they outnumbered the RAF two-to-one, the RAF held off German attacks. Although there was massive damage and loss of life, Germany didn't achieve the conquest they were after. This has been seen as one of the biggest turning points of the war, buoying British morale and shaking German confidence.

The Blitz

The Blitz is probably the most famous thing to happen in Britain during World War Two. It refers to the several months that German air forces spent bombing major city centres (mostly London) in order to terrorize and kill citizens. The name *Blitz* is short for *Blitzkrieg*, which means "lightning war" in German, referring to the massive use of bombs and explosives.

While the Blitz refers to attacks on many industries as

well as cities, in Britain, it's best known for its effect on London.

During the Blitz, London civilians (especially children) were evacuated to rural areas to try to get out of the way of the bombs, but not everyone could leave. Bomb shelters became a fixture of every home and neighbourhood, and nightly air raid sirens signalled to citizens that they needed to get underground or else be killed.

The German air force, or *Luftwaffe*, dropped about 41,000 tonnes of bombs on Britain during the Blitz, and estimated death counts are around 40,000 civilians (not to mention military lives lost), and more than a million houses were destroyed in London alone.

Rations on the Home Front

World War One was the first war in which British civilians had to really get involved in the war effort, and World War Two took that to an even higher level. From producing supplies in factories to giving up material items that could be more useful in the military, people in Britain were expected to "do their part" towards the war effort.

Laws were put in place about what materials could be used for activities at home. These laws were called *rationing laws*.

Food was scarce, and the types that were available

were things like tins of spam, crackers, canned fruit, and breakfast cereals. Fresh fruits and vegetables were around but very expensive, and there was a thriving black market for every type of food you couldn't get legally.

Other things were rationed too—rubber, metal, and even silk and nylon, which were used to make parachutes! The rations on silk and nylon meant that women couldn't wear stockings and were actually encouraged to send their old stockings in to the governments to make parachutes out of.

No woman would want to be accused of withholding supplies from the government, but you couldn't just go stockings-less in the 1940s! So a popular practice of faking stockings sprung up. Women rubbed gravy all over their legs to darken their skin and then drew fake seams up the backs of their legs with eyeliner pencils. Considering that the gravy rations they were getting were little powder packets, it really wasn't that much of a waste.

Mad Jack Churchill

Lest you think that the only British figures of note were the Prime Ministers and the Nazi supporters, let's talk about the famous John Malcolm Thorpe Flemming "Jack" Churchill, a British soldier and the only man in the British military to kill enemy soldiers with a bow and arrow.

In the 1930s, Churchill had a minor movie career and went to the World Archery Championships, but in 1939, like any able-bodied Briton, he joined the military. Churchill's son claimed that when the Germans were approaching Churchill at L'Épinette, he said, "I will shoot that first German with an arrow" … and he did. He then showed up to the Battle of Dunkirk by bicycle, bow and arrow in tow, and got a few more good shots in before being flown back to England.

With a flair for the dramatic, Churchill also enjoyed playing the bagpipes during military campaigns, using them as a call to action for his fellow Commandos. He happened to be playing them when he was captured by the Germans in Yugoslavia, but don't worry, he escaped through a drain pipe and started a four hundred-mile walk towards the Baltic coast. He was picked up by the Germans again, escaped when they were being handed over between two groups of soldiers, and then walked another ninety-three miles to Verona, where he finally found an American unit that took him to safety.

In a massive oversight by Hollywood, Jack Churchill has not yet been the subject of any movies. But if you want to see him on the silver screen, you can watch his 1952 film *Ivanhoe*, where he has a brief role as, of course, an archer.

The Battle of France

Remember that when the Treaty of Versailles was signed, the French government complained that they were the country most vulnerable to retaliation from Germany, and they turned out to be right.

When Germany invaded Poland in 1939, France immediately declared war and invaded Saarland, Germany's western territory, in retaliation. France had made an alliance with Poland in 1921, but they were motivated as much by fear as by their responsibility to the Poles. They knew that they would be next.

Over the next year, Germany proved its military power by conquering Poland with hardly any struggle. Their style of warfare was new, fast-paced, and difficult to contain. At the beginning of May of 1940, only nine months after invading Poland, Germany finished up with Poland and turned their attention to France.

It didn't take long before the German army broke through French defences, and by the end of May, the Allied forces were evacuating their soldiers from the battle. France was defeated at the beginning of June, shaken by the speed of their defeat and shocked by Britain's inability to protect them. On June 17, 1940, the French President of the Council, delivered a speech to the French people telling them, "It is necessary to cease to fight." France was resigned to German occupation.

Vichy France

The German army took control of the northern part of France, but things got a little more complicated in the southern part. The south of France was called the French State, and was run by a Marshal named Philippe Pétain, mainly out of the town of Vichy, hence the name of the state, Vichy France.

Officially, when it was formed in 1940, Vichy was a neutral state. Pétain had been a war hero in World War One, and had some pretty strong ideas about why France had fallen to the Germans so quickly. Specifically, he claimed that it was because France had become so weak under the Third Republic, which was the governmental system that had been in place since the 1870s.

The Third Republic had been developed as a transitional government after France had lost the Franco-Prussian War (another war between France and Germany) in the 1870s. However, while it was only meant to be in place for a couple of years, it never quite went away.

Pétain thought that the Third Republic government had weakened the state because it focussed on democracy instead of authority. So, when he set up Vichy France as his own personal government, he put an authoritarian regime in place and did away with all that democratic nonsense.

Pétain was also a pretty big fan of Hitler. He didn't have any hesitations about siding with Germany, even though Vichy France was officially neutral. He also adopted the Nazi racial policies in Vichy France, and approved a eugenics program that sanctioned killing or sterilizing people who were considered racially impure.

Officially, Pétain had every right to side with Germany, and his reasoning could even have been considered pretty solid, since the Germans had already shown themselves to have the superior military. Trying to make peace with them wasn't totally unreasonable. When it was formed, countries all over the world recognized Vichy France as legitimate. Unfortunately for Pétain, Vichy France ended up as less of an ally and more of a puppet of the Nazi government.

Occupied France

In the south, there was Vichy France. Vichy France was obviously in the Nazis' pocket, but it was, in theory, a free and sovereign state, just one that happened to agree with German policies and have an alliance with them. Nothing unsovereign about that!

Things were a little different in the north. Alsace-Lorraine, which had gone back and forth between French and German control for decades, went back into German hands. Before 1942, only about half of France was controlled by Germany (and a small bit of the southeastern border was controlled by Italy), but as the years went on, more and more of the country fell under German military occupation.

The German army took this opportunity to get back at France for its harsh treatment after World War One. They demanded that occupied France pay the costs of their army, which was about 40 million *Reichsmark*, or 66 million modern American dollars, every single day. To make things even worse, Germany made up an exchange rate between French Franks and German Reichsmark, claiming that one Reichsmark was worth twenty Franks. If France couldn't pay up, then the German army got the money by plundering towns and seizing anything of value, including food.

As if that wasn't bad enough, Germany cut off most of France's trade with any allied country and held most of their workforce as prisoners of war, so there was no way for them to produce more. There were shortages of supplies all over France that made Britain's rations look positively generous.

Malgré-Nous

As if it wasn't bad enough that France was occupied and that the whole country was suffering from incredible shortages because of the reparations the German army was demanding, there was another danger for young men in occupied France. They were being conscripted into the German army.

Since occupied France was *basically* part of Germany (at least, according to the Germans), young able-bodied men were expected to serve in the military and would face consequences if they refused. Shockingly, there weren't many French men voluntarily signing up for the SS, so, as far as the German army was concerned, it was only reasonable to force them into action.

Most of the French soldiers were sent to especially dangerous parts of the war zone, like the Eastern Front. Others were put into the *Waffen-SS*, the more prestigious part of Germany's armed forces. If they refused to serve, their entire families would be deported (or worse).

Malgré-nous is French for "against our will." Many young men forced into service escaped to join the French Resistance or fled to neutral Switzerland, but doing so was risky. If they were caught, they would be executed, and even if they weren't, their families could face the consequences. Things didn't get better after the war either, when they were accused of being traitors to France, even though they would have been killed if they had done anything differently.

The French Resistance

France was not just lying back and taking it while Germany conquered them! There were all sorts of efforts in France to destabilize the German occupiers. They were doing everything from forming guerrilla warfare groups to publishing newspapers with firsthand information about the Nazi regime in them.

Unlike the strictly regulated German army (which, of course, didn't allow anyone into the high ranks unless they were both politically and racially "approved"), the resistance leader Emmanuel d'Astier de la Vigerie described the French Resistance as being made up of outcasts. These included Gaullists (French patriots), communists and socialists, far-right groups that didn't like having Germany control Vichy France, Roman Catholic priests, students and academics, people from other countries (including anti-Nazi Germans), and, of course, Jewish citizens.

While there was resistance from the beginning, it wasn't until 1942 that the French Resistance became organized. Up until then, they hadn't been able to make contact with the Allies, so all their efforts were pretty limited. But as time went on, Allied countries were able to offer support, and resistance became more unified and better organized all across France.

Free French Forces

A little more organized and a little more focussed on war tactics than the French Resistance, the Free French Forces were created in 1940, and rejected both German authority and the authority of Vichy France. The authority they did support was General Charles de Gaulle, who demanded that France resist Nazi occupation at every term.

On June 18, 1940, de Gaulle made a speech over the BBC radio (in French), saying, "Believe me, I who am speaking to you with the full knowledge of the facts and who can tell you that nothing is lost for France. The same means that overcame us can bring us victory one day." Winston Churchill personally ensured that it was broadcasted in England, despite resistance from the British cabinet, who were worried that the speech would provoke the Nazis.

While at first the Free French Forces were a very small army made of volunteers, their numbers swelled as Resistance members joined them, and they also merged with the *Armée d'Afrique*, which was an army recruited from French colonies in North Africa.

De Gaulle was accused of treason by Vichy France, but that didn't stop him from leading an impressive army and being hailed as a national hero by French people since.

The Liberation of Paris

Paris had been under Nazi control from the beginning, and in August 1944, the Parisians had finally had enough.

Non-French military leaders didn't consider liberating Paris to be very important. After all, it had already been under Nazi control for four years. Hitler had also made the order to destroy Paris if the Allies attacked it. Everyone was wary of doing anything to provoke him.

However, Charles de Gaulle wasn't interested in waiting around for the "right time" to make a move. He sent a small group of soldiers to Paris, informing them that the entire Free France force would be there the next day, and he followed through on his promise. On August 25, 1944, an army of Spanish soldiers broke into Paris, followed by the French and American divisions. It took less than a day before Choltitz, the German military governor of Paris, surrendered.

And, despite his threats, he didn't destroy Paris, although there have been a lot of arguments about whether he chose not to do it of his own free will, was convinced by the allied forces not to, or simply didn't have the opportunity to give the orders.

RANDOM FACTS

1. Shortages in Britain were so severe that British soldiers were rationed three sheets of toilet paper per day.

2. During the food rationing, one British biologist became so hungry that he ate a laboratory rat.

3. The princess of England was a driver and mechanic during World War Two. You might know her name… Elizabeth.

4. Hitler apparently hated lipstick and thought it detracted from natural beauty. As such, British women were encouraged to wear bright red lipstick and overdrawn lips! Even while other cosmetics were rationed, red lipstick was considered important enough to morale to not be restricted.

5. During the Blitz, British officials expected widespread panic, suicide attempts, and mental illness. They even opened special clinics for shock victims. However, those clinics closed because the demand was so low. British civilians were so determined to get through the war that they did not allow their minds to deteriorate during the bombings.

6. The London Underground system (colloquially called "The Tube") was one of the best and most popular bombing shelters. About 150 thousand people slept there every night.

7. Remember the scene in the movie *Zoolander* where a conspiracy is revealed, that every great assassination in history was carried out by male models? Three guesses what Jack Churchill's job was before World War Two. That's right: male model.

8. Germany got famous for its crazy ideas for weapons and tactics, but Britain had its own fair share. Project Habukkuk was a British plan to build an aircraft carrier entirely out of ice and wood pulp. It was planned in Alberta, Canada, (where temperatures regularly fall below -40 degrees Celsius) but was eventually shelved for being expensive and impractical.

9. In 1940, France had a bigger military than Germany, with more manpower and more weaponry.

10. In spite of France's superior numbers, the Battle of France lasted only 46 days before they were crushed by the German forces.

11. The French Resistance adopted the Cross of Lorraine as their symbol, a cross with two horizontal bars. They weren't the first ones to use

the Cross of Lorraine. A variation of the two-armed cross appears on the coat of arms of Joan of Arc!

12. Prior to World War Two, feminism was popular in France, but both the Nazis and Pétain had pretty strict ideas about the roles of women (that is, they should stay at home and make a lot of babies). While the French Resistance wasn't exactly pro-feminist, some women did join it to try to prevent a backwards slide into limiting ideas about womanhood.

13. The Southern United States (especially Louisiana) had a large Cajun population, made up of French Canadians (or *Acadians*) who had been deported almost two hundred years earlier. Cajuns in the United States army could collaborate with the French in order to provide American support to the Resistance.

14. One of the ways that the French resisted the Germans was economically. French coal miners went on strike, stopping the deliveries of coal that they were being forced to send to Germany.

15. Winston Churchill was elected Prime Minister of Britain once the war broke out. He was known for his brash personality, which was why he was such a popular choice. Urban legend has it that a woman once told him, "If you were my husband,

I would poison your food." To which he responded, "Madam, if I were your husband, I would eat it."

16. One French resistance fighter died from eating plastic explosives, which he mistook for cheese.

17. Spain was supposed to be neutral during World War Two, but they had no qualms about helping liberate France from the Germans.

18. Muslims were not targeted by the Nazis in the way that Jews were. The Mosque of Paris gave Jewish citizens Muslim identification papers to protect them.

19. In 1940, the armistice between France and Germany was signed in the same railway carriage in which Germany had signed their surrender after World War One.

20. Before World War Two, France was in the same time zone as England. When Germany occupied it, they forced France to change its time zone to be the same as the one in Germany. This is still how it is today.

Test Yourself – Questions and Answers

1) What does *Blitzkrieg* mean?

   a. Pre-emptive strike
   b. Lightning war
   c. Night bombings

2) Who was *not* a British Prime Minister during World War Two?

   a. Wallis Simpson
   b. Neville Chamberlain
   c. Winston Churchill

3) Which of the above was *not* done by Jack Churchill?

   a. Played "March of the Cameron Men" on the bagpipes before charging into battle
   b. Escaped a concentration camp through a drain pipe
   c. Appeared as himself in the film *Dunkirk*

4) What symbol did the French Resistance adopt?

   a. The Fleur-de-lis
   b. The Cross of Lorraine
   c. The tricolour flag

5) What was Vichy France's *official* political stance?

   a. It supported the Allied powers, like Britain
   b. It was neutral
   d. It supported the Axis powers, like Germany

Answers

1. c
2. a
3. c
4. b
5. b

CHAPTER THREE

THE UNITED STATES AND SOVIET UNION AT WAR

Just like in World War One, the United States took a little longer to join in the war than some other countries did. Especially after the unmitigated disaster that was World War One, the States weren't exactly enthusiastic about getting involved in another European land war. However, when Japan bombed Pearl Harbour, the States went all in.

On the other hand, the Soviet Union ended up being one of the biggest players in World War Two, suffering the biggest losses in their army and generally taking the brunt of Germany's military aggression. They were pretty furious at the Nazi army (and a little bit resentful towards the other allies, who they sometimes felt like "weren't pulling their weight"), and were ready to use any means necessary to decimate the German army.

Since when the war ended it was the United States

and the Soviet Union that appeared as the biggest superpowers on the world stage, it only makes sense to learn about them together. They were allies, but they were always a little bit uneasy with each other, so keep that tension in mind while you learn about their roles in the war!

The War with Japan

While Germany was the main focus on British military efforts, the States were more concerned with Japan. Not exactly surprising, since Japan was the country that bombed them while Germany had been staying out of their way! A lot of American war propaganda ended up focussing on the Japanese and the war in the Pacific, rather than on Hitler and the European war. This was different from the general attitude in Europe, which was that they should deal with Germany first, before they started worrying about what was happening in Japan.

For around half a year, the American military floundered, while Japan sustained success after success. However, in June 1942, the Americans won the Battle of Midway and turned the tides on the Japanese.

In the Battle of Midway, Japan was relying on the element of surprise that had served them so well with Pearl Harbour, but their codes were broken, and the Americans discovered when and where the attack would be taking place, and ambushed the Japanese navy. They destroyed all four of Japan's aircraft carriers while losing only one themselves.

The defeat was so significant for Japan that the Japanese military began to struggle to replace its lost soldiers and weaponry, putting it at a disadvantage for the rest of the war.

The United States' Super Powers

From the perspective of the Europeans who were suffering during World War Two, the United States seemed like the Superman of countries—nothing could hurt it. For one thing, North America had massive natural resources compared to European countries. Not exactly hard, considering that the United States is almost ten million square kilometers, compared to France's six and a half hundred thousand square kilometers – but still impressive. Canada is bigger than the United States in terms of land mass and at least as rich in natural resources, but its population was a fraction of the US's, and it wasn't nearly as industrially developed at the time, making the States a much bigger power.

But on top of that, the United States are separated from Europe by thousands of miles of ocean. While it wasn't hard for the Nazis to invade France or bomb out Britain, it would have been a massive investment for them to even get planes all the way to the United

States, much less actually drop bombs on the United States' economic or political centres, which were also spread out pretty widely compared to Europe's!

Japan got close enough to Hawaii to make an attack, but Hawaii is still two and a half thousand miles from the mainland United States. Even then, the bombing of Pearl Harbour was a much less sustained effort than the attacks that Germany made on London. It took more resources and planning, and was harder to replicate.

The United States seemed like a superhero country in World War Two, but its super powers weren't anything mysterious—it was huge, and it was far away.

The Fireside Chats

Even before the US entered the war, public sentiment definitely favoured the Allied powers (like Britain) over the Axis powers (like Germany). People didn't yet know exactly what Hitler's "war machine" looked like, and they definitely didn't know that he was planning on killing millions of Jewish civilians and other unlucky groups, but they still knew that they didn't like where the European fascists were going. They saw it as being against American values – and the United States has always been very interested in values!

Part of the reason that the public was so anti-Nazi (in general) was thanks to President Franklin Delano Roosevelt, who had developed a very popular radio program called the "Fireside Chats" over the previous decade.

Roosevelt started doing his Fireside Chats during the Great Depression, when he was aware that most people didn't know what was going on, except that things were bad, and their ignorance was breeding fear and anger. The point of the Fireside Chats was to update the people of the United States on politics, from the most reliable source (the President himself), in a calm, thoughtful, and casual way, like they were just sitting by a fire and chatting! They were crucial in diffusing the tensions that were happening in the States during the Depression by keeping people informed, and they did the same thing during World War Two.

When things started to get ugly in Europe, Roosevelt dedicated time in his fireside chats to explaining the situation in Europe. Of course, his chats had a lot to do with his opinion, and his opinion was definitely pro-Britain! To the United States population, he explained why it was a good idea to support Britain rather than Germany, and most people were quick to agree.

The Undeclared War Against China

The United States were also one of very few countries that had any interest at all in helping China when Japan was attacking it. However, in 1937, when the Second Sino-Japanese War broke out (as discussed in

Chapter One), the United States' neutrality acts were still preventing them from aiding any country at war. As we now know, those neutrality acts were not long for this wold, but at the time, Roosevelt knew that there would be an outcry from American isolationists if he helped a country for war.

Lucky for Roosevelt (and China), the Second Sino-Japanese war was never officially declared. The Japanese military didn't seem to think it was worth the trouble to officially *tell* China that they were attacking them when it was so much easier to just go ahead and attack (the official explanation was that China's government was too fractured for a message to be sent). However, because the war was undeclared and considered an "incident," the US had every right to send aid to China, and they did. Public opinion was generally in China's favour, and Roosevelt didn't suffer much bad press when he decided to send aid to Chiang Kai-shek, the leader of the Republic of China.

The Peacetime Draft

In 1940, the States were still trying to avoid getting involved in the war in Europe, but it was becoming obvious that unless something about the situation changed, they'd have to join the war at some point. So, the American government created its first-ever peacetime draft—drafting an army before they even declared war.

In theory, just because a country starts calling up soldiers and creating an army, it doesn't mean they're planning on going to war. Today, lots of countries have mandatory military service, and we aren't expecting all of them to break out in fights at any minute. But given the climate of 1940, this was a sign from the United States that they were willing to start fighting, if they needed to.

Technically, there's *still* a draft in the United States, but it's a little different. All able men *might* be called up at any time, if there's a war, but they don't have to do any kind of military training *until* there's a war, so they're not *really* in the army *yet*. In 1940, the United States seemed to be saying, "well, we're not *planning* on entering the war, but just in case, we've got a couple hundred thousand trained soldiers ready to go."

Bataan, 1942

The bombing at Pearl Harbour is an internationally recognized American tragedy, with approximately 2,400 Americans killed. But thousands of American (and Filipino) soldiers also died after the United States' ill-fated surrender at Bataan. They didn't die in a bombing but in a long, brutal walk known as the Bataan Death March.

Bataan is a peninsula in the Philippine islands, and before World War Two, it had been under American control. As part of their expansionist project, the Japanese military decided to capture Bataan in the spring of 1942. They fought for three months against the American and Filipino troops that were stationed there, but the American army in Bataan was not receiving any aid from the Navy or the Air Force, and after three months, they were forced to surrender.

The troops had been starving and diseased while they were under attack, and things only got worse once they surrendered. The Japanese military grouped the Americans and Filipinos into groups of 100, then started to march them sixty-five miles across the peninsula towards a prisoner-of-war camp.

The heat was extreme, the troops were already weakened from the long battle, and the capturing Japanese army had no problem beating the troops or even stabbing them with bayonets if they became too weak to walk. The lucky ones survived to the camps, where they were also beaten and mistreated, succumbed to disease, and were starved. While the exact numbers are unknown, 75,000 troops were captured, and the death toll was undoubtedly massive.

Operation Husky

America started its activities in World War Two in the Pacific, fighting against Japan. Then it joined the British fighting in North Africa, and *then*, around 1943, instead of attacking the Germans who were occupying France, the United States decided to invade Sicily, which was part of Italy and controlled by the Italian fascists, who were Hitler's allies. This invasion was given the code name "Operation Husky."

The US attack on Sicily involved both water and air attacks, which weakened the Italian forces before they even started attacking on land.

This attack achieved a few different things. Firstly, once Sicily was captured, Allied ships could use that space for sea travel, taking routes through the Mediterranean Sea to get from one side of Europe to the other, rather than needing to go by land. For another, it unseated the Italian dictator Benito Mussolini. It also distracted the Germans from their attacks on the Eastern Front, as they diverted their troops to help the Italians, weakening their overall strategy.

The GI Influx

In 1942, when American soldiers landed in Britain, they were well-funded, enthusiastic, and—in a word—*cool*. Their wages and rations were much higher than the tight British funds, and they brought cigarettes and cans of Coca-Cola, plus plenty of partying spirit.

Most British people at that time hadn't met many (if any) Americans, except maybe if they had served in a neighbouring regiment during World War One. Cowboys (especially financially successful cowboys) had been very "in" during the late Victorian period, so most images of Americans were gun-slinging, highly attractive, self-made millionaires. One British teenager recalls thinking that Americans would be "tall, immaculately dressed, [and] run about the country shooting Indians."

The Americans who did show up to Britain weren't exactly like he imagined, but they did inject some spirit and patriotism into down-and-out England when it was very much needed. They also flaunted their money, held parties, played jazz music, flirted with English girls, and bought them expensive presents. The stereotype of the "wild west" man didn't exactly disappear!

D-Day

Believe it or not, D-Day, the invasion of Normandy in 1944, was the United States' first real offensive *directly* against the Nazis in Europe. It's also one of the most famous military campaigns in all of history. It was the largest invasion ever conducted by sea and marked the beginning of the end for the Axis powers.

The allied troops landed in Normandy (France) at midnight on June 6th, and the armoured divisions arrived early that morning. At that time, Germany had the upper hand. The beaches that they landed on were covered in barbed wire and mines, and soldiers were stationed behind the walls, shooting at them. However, after almost a week, the Allied troops had captured all of the beaches and were then able to expand further and further into mainland France once they had their foothold on the coast.

At least 10,000 Allied soldiers were estimated to have died in the D-Day campaigns, although only around 4,500 were confirmed. The estimates for German deaths are lower—between 4,000 and 9,000. However, even with the massive casualties, this was the Allies' greatest success, and things would only go better from then on.

Moving on to the East: Spheres of Influence

Now that you know all about the Americans in World War Two, let's take a look over to the Eastern front, where the Soviet Union (Russia, and the countries that had gotten on board with Russia's brand of communist government) was having a really bad time.

When World War Two started, the Soviet Union *really* didn't want to fight against Germany. In the summer of 1939, they signed a pact promising that neither country would invade the other. It also divided up the territories that both Germany and Russia had claims to (like Romania, Finland, and, of course, Poland) into what were called the German and Soviet "spheres of influence."

A "sphere of influence" is a territory (like a country or state) that's not ruled by another country, but is affected by its culture, economy, and politics. Think of it like the younger sibling of the bigger country. The bigger country isn't *technically* the boss, but if the bigger country wants it to do something, there's a pretty good chance that the smaller company will want to do it.

However, even though the Nazis and Soviets took the time to make this pact, they violated it almost immediately, and it was a free-for-all with both the German and Soviet armies going after each other's spheres of influence with no hesitation.

The Battle of Stalingrad

The Battle of Stalingrad might be one of the most famous battles in all of military history. It was a battle between the Nazi and Soviet armies over the South Russian city of Stalingrad.

In August 1942, the Germans decided it was time to capture this strategically important city and used the same tactic that they were using against Britain: aerial bombing that left the city in ruins and cost massive civilian life. They also used a technique called "house-to-house fighting," which takes advantage of houses and buildings for laying ambushes and makes the actual strength of each side's weaponry less important.

The German army was using two of its partner armies,

Romania and Hungary, to protect it on either side while it attacked the city. These armies were much less powerful than the German army, which was why they were being used as protection in the first place, but the Soviet army took advantage of that. After four months of fighting, in which they were being slowly overwhelmed and pushed back by the Germans, they launched an attack on the Romanian and Hungarian army, and by overpowering them were able to surround the German army.

The Surrender at Stalingrad

Hitler ordered his armies to stay in Stalingrad, saying he would give them supplies by air. It was just like a medieval siege. The German and Axis armies were supposed to stay inside the city, refuse to allow it to be captured, and wait for the Soviet troops to become exhausted.

However, while sieges might have worked in the Middle Ages, they aren't the best technique in a twentieth-century war. The Soviets had a distinct advantage and no plans of backing down.

After two months of fighting, the few Axis troops that were still alive were ready to surrender to the Soviets. They knew that there was no winning. By now, it was also deep into the Russian winter, and the German soldiers were ill-prepared. After all, they'd invaded in summer and only had their summer uniforms.

Hitler either didn't understand or didn't care about the dire situation. He ordered his armies not to surrender, and then, when the field marshal, Friedrich Paulus, sent word that they were going to, Hitler ordered him to commit suicide if he was captured.

To this gory order from Hitler, Paulus replied, with nerve that would make Jack Churchill proud, "I have no intention of shooting myself for this Bohemian corporal."

The Oath of the Red Army

Since the political situation in Russia wasn't so great even outside of the war, leaders were concerned that soldiers conscripted into the army would be tempted to defect, flee the military, or share information with the other side. This was a fairly reasonable concern. The zone they needed to protect was huge and surrounded by the enemies. It didn't help that death tolls were enormous. So, they created an oath that all soldiers were required to take at the end of training, focussing on the main pots of their communist ideology to try to keep soldiers focussed on the moral reasons for going to war.

Gordon Rottman translated the Oath of the Red Army as:

> I, [soldier's name], a citizen of the Union of the Soviet Socialist Republics, entering into the ranks

of the Red Army of the Workers and Peasants', take this oath and solemnly promise to be a honest, brave, disciplined, vigilant fighter, staunchly to protect military and state secrets, and unquestioningly to obey all military regulations and orders of commanders and superiors.

I promise conscientiously to study military affairs, in every way to protect state secrets and state property, and to my last breath to be faithful to the people, the Soviet Motherland, and the Workers-Peasants' Government.

I am always prepared on order of the Workers and Peasants Government to rise to the defense of my Motherland, the Union of Soviet Socialist Republics; and as a fighting man of the Red Army of Workers and Peasants', I promise to defend it bravely, skillfully, with dignity and honor, sparing neither my blood nor my life itself for the achievement of total victory over our enemies.

If by evil intent I should violate this, my solemn oath, then let the severe punishment of Soviet law and the total hatred and contempt of the working classes befall me.

The Polish Grave

Lest you think that the Soviets were any friendlier than the Nazis just because they were on the Allied side of the war, they were just as willing to massacre their enemies as the Germans were. Joseph Stalin, the leader of the Soviet Union, actually may have had a much higher body count than Hitler did. He certainly wasn't a big fan of Poland either, especially Poles who wanted to be independent from both the Nazi *and* the Soviet spheres of influence.

He wasn't afraid to show it either—by having Polish soldiers and civilians alike slaughtered.

When a Polish general asked Stalin where the Polish officers that Stalin had "liberated" were, Stalin claimed that the Soviet army had "lost track" of them, until a group of railway workers found them in a mass grave.

Both the Soviets and the Nazis tried to push the blame on each other, with the Nazis using it to sow distrust among the Allies and the Soviets trying to blame it on German soldiers. The Nazis predicted that this was probably going to happen and were furious, because, for once, they *weren't* the ones who did it! It was a source of controversy for decades.

However, in 1990, the Soviets finally admitted that they were the ones who massacred the Polish soldiers.

The Battle of Berlin

The Battle of Berlin was the last major battle in Europe in World War Two, between the Soviet Union and

Germany. By this time, the Soviet army was about three times the size of the Nazi army, and the amount of artillery dedicated to the battle was similarly enormous.

The citizens of Berlin knew that the end was nigh, and the Nazis knew it as well. They put children and elderly citizens into the front lines of the battle, hoping it would dissuade the Soviet army from wholesale destruction, but it didn't. The Soviet army drove tanks into the city, practically flattening it, and dropped over two million shells on Berlin and surrounding areas.

Russia lost about 80,000 soldiers in battle, while only about half of the 15,000 Germans were killed during it. It was a decisive Allied victory and marked the end of the German regime.

RANDOM FACTS

1. In the 1930s, when the US were making decisions about whether to aid China or not, it helped that the Chinese-American writer Pearl S. Buck just happened to have one of the bestselling novels in the country, *The Good Earth*. Buck wrote about the horrors in China and aroused public sympathy and support.

2. During World War Two, the United States didn't want *any* German-sounding food on their menus. Unfortunately, one of the most popular American meals, the hamburger, is named after the German city of Hamburg. Americans didn't want to give up that delicacy, so they started calling them "liberty steaks" instead.

3. They also started calling "frankfurters" (named after the German city of Frankfurt) "hot dogs." This one caught on a little better than "liberty steaks."

4. Canada declared war on Japan after the bombing of Pearl Harbour too, one day before the United States got around to it.

5. If we adjust for inflation, in modern American dollars, World War Two cost the United States

about 4.5 trillion dollars.

6. John R. McKinney, an American soldier in the 1945 Philippines campaign, fought off a hundred Japanese soldiers by himself.

7. Until 1944, there were always more American military servicemen in the Pacific fighting Japan than there were in Europe fighting Germany.

8. The United States Marine Corps used the acronyms BAM and HAM for women and men (respectively) in the Marines. They stood for "Broad-Assed Marines" and "Hairy-Assed Marines."

9. The pact between the Nazis and Soviets regarding which countries were under each other's spheres of influence wasn't revealed until 1989.

10. Soviet soldiers shouted the war cry *Ura!* when they attacked. It's a traditional Russian battle cry, originating from an old Turkish word meaning "kill!"

11. In the 1930s, the Soviet Union was working on a design for fighter aircraft, but they couldn't build a powerful enough engine to get it off the ground. The engineers did know of one company that was making sufficiently powerful engines—Rolls Royce. They appealed to Stalin to ask the British to sell them some Rolls Royce engines. Stalin

pointed out that the British were currently their enemies but gave it a shot anyway, and yes, the British sold them the engines.

12. Russia had the largest number of casualties of any country in World War Two, with over 21 million soldiers and civilians killed.

13. The war with Russia wasn't great for Germany either—80% of all German soldiers who were killed in World War Two died on the Eastern Front, fighting Russia.

14. And things were bad for the people the Russians captured too. 85% of everyone interned in the Russian prisoner-of-war camps died.

15. The Russian army was the first in the world to use paratroopers.

16. The blood transfusion was invented during World War Two, and saved hundreds of thousands of lives.

17. The Soviet army has been accused of an awful lot of war crimes... including the rapes of two million German women.

18. The United States Medal of Honour was awarded to 464 Americans, 266 posthumously.

19. A Soviet woman named Roza Shanina worked as a sniper and killed at least 54 enemies.

20. The classic American snack food Cheetos were invented in 1943 as a way to freeze-dry cheese for humid climates.

Test Yourself – Questions and Answers

1) Which of these events didn't happen in the year 1942?

   a. The Battle of Stalingrad

   b. The Battle of Midway

   c. The Battle of Berlin

2) What did Friedrich Paulus call Hitler?

   a. A "Bohemian corporal"

   b. A "Viennese postcard artist"

   c. A "Bavarian madman"

3) What is a sphere of influence?

   a. A country's colonial possessions

   b. Countries affected by the culture, politics, and economics of another country

   c. A military experiment that protected soldiers in an invisible bubble

4) What was Russia's strategy in the Battle of Stalingrad

   a. Barricade themselves in the city, like a Medieval siege

   b. Cut off the German army from its allies and surround it

   c. Flatten the city of Stalingrad with tanks

5) What did Americans call hamburgers, to avoid being associated with the German city of Hamburg?

a. Patriotism patties
b. Freedom sandwiches
c. Liberty steaks

Answers

1. c
2. a
3. b
4. b
5. c

CHAPTER FOUR

GERMANY AND JAPAN AT WAR

Germany and Japan were the two biggest Axis powers. Italy came in as a close third, and Hungary, Romania, and a variety of other countries sided with them too, but Germany and Japan were the most powerful and the most ambitious. With big plans and big weapons, these two countries ended up wreaking havoc all over the world.

This chapter will feature a couple of facts from other Axis powers, but mostly, we're going to learn about the big two: Germany and Japan. They were the countries that were most aggressive with their war campaign. They had a lot in common—like wanting to expand to have big territories, and feeling like they had been oppressed by their surrounding countries—but they also had some pretty big differences. The Japanese didn't care very much about the Jewish population, and Germany wasn't interested in claiming land in the Pacific.

While the Axis power armies committed horrible war crimes and have (not wrongly) gone down in history as the "bad guys," they weren't just sitting around scheming about how to be evil, and not everyone in their countries agreed with the leaders. Read on to find out about what was happening in Nazi Germany and Imperial Japan, and how everything managed to go so wrong.

Verbrennt man auch am Ende Menschen

Hitler got started early in trying to weed out dissenting voices. In 1933, six whole years before invading Poland, the Nazi party arranged a series of book burnings at universities all across Germany. Students and professors alike made bonfires of books that were considered "anti-German."

Some of the books that ended up in these fires were by English language authors like Jack London and H. G. Wells. Others were by Jewish writers like Sigmund Freud and Albert Einstein. Some of them were popular novels. Others were serious scholarly works and textbooks.

Before the age of the internet, and especially in a country where book printing and selling were both expensive and governmentally controlled, burning books was an extremely efficient way to cut people off from information that might have made them think anything the Nazis didn't want them to think. People reading the works of Freud or Einstein might have more positive, humanized views of Jewish people, and reading English books would make it a lot harder to get people to see America and Britain as the enemy. The book burnings were energetic events that got people excited about the Nazi party and the act of "purifying" their minds by destroying "impure" books.

Don't forget the famous quote from the nineteenth century German poet Heinrich Heine, a hundred years before Hitler: "*Dort wo man Bücher verbrennt, verbrennt man auch am Ende Menschen*"... meaning "Where they have burned books, they will end in burning people."

The Night of the Long Knives

Also known as Operation Hummingbird, or the *Röhm Putsch*, the Night of the Long Knives was a group of political assassinations at the end of June 1934, against Hitler's political enemies in Germany or anyone who he thought might try to limit his power.

Among those killed were the leaders of the *Sturmabteilung*, which was the Nazi paramilitary organization. These leaders had been Hitler's allies and supporters, but some of them also held communist sympathies (which Hitler would not allow), and many more simply didn't approve of the obvious road towards dictatorship that the Nazis were on. Remember, the Nazis were the National *Socialist* party, and many people in the *Sturmabteilung* were still more interested in socialist economic change than in totalitarianism and ethnic cleansing. Hitler was also worried that the *Sturmebteilung* was too independent, and that their tendency to engage in street violence would damage his image.

Other people were killed too, including leftists, conservatives who supported Germany's old government, and anyone who had ever voiced anti-Nazi sentiment. They also killed the politician who had stopped Hitler's attempt to seize power in Munich eleven years earlier.

It's unknown exactly how many people were killed during the Night of the Long Knives. It was at least 85, but some estimates are as high as a thousand, and another thousand people were arrested by the *Schutzstaffel* and *Gestapo*, the secret police.

The Salon Kitty

If there's one thing that wealthy, stressed politicians can't resist, it's a good prostitute. The general of the SS, Reinhard Heydrich, bought out the famous "Salon Kitty" brothel in Berlin in 1939, with the plan to invite high-ranking politicians, both German and foreign, and casually extract information from them while they were visiting the prostitutes.

The owner of the brothel, Kitty Schmidt, was forced to cooperate with the Nazis after it was revealed that she had been giving money to refugees. She handed over her brothel to them to turn it into a Nazi spy hotspot.

Every woman in the brothel was a trained spy. The advertisement for prostitutes read "Wanted are women and girls who are intelligent, multilingual, nationalistically minded, and man-crazy." The rooms were equipped with listening devices, and the women were required to make a report after every encounter, telling them about any secrets their men might have spilled.

There is no shortage of scandalous stories about the goings-on at Salon Kitty, like one SS general's request for a 21-person all-night orgy, or Joseph Goebbels' alleged interest in watching "lesbian displays." Remember, homosexuality was considered grounds for going to a concentration camp!

Sexy Propaganda

As if it wasn't weird enough that the Nazis had special spy brothels, there were other ways that sex was being used for the war effort by countries on every side. Several countries, but especially Germany, attempted to use sexually explicit propaganda to decrease enemy morale. It was a technique that was part of the craze for "psychological operations" that preyed on the enemy's mind, using new techniques from psychology and psychiatry, and although it ended up being wildly unsuccessful, it has given us some interesting pieces of history.

Thousands of leaflets were dropped on enemy soldiers that tried to use sexual fears, such as fear of rape or inadequacy, to discourage the troops. For example, the Nazis created leaflets that showed peaceful, pastoral scenes, but when held up to the light, revealed images of women being raped by Soviet soldiers, to try to draw wedges between the Soviets and the other allies. (Of course, the Soviet army did rape a lot of women, so this one is more honest propaganda than most of the others).

They also created a series of drawings of beautiful young women being seduced by overweight and opulently dressed stereotypes of Jewish men, with captions like "the girl you left behind." These were meant to convince Allied soldiers that, while they were out risking their lives, their wives and girlfriends were cheating on them with the very people they were trying to protect.

On a similar vein, leaflets were distributed to the British showing women having sex with American soldiers. This preyed on their fear of popularity of American GIs in Britain, which we discussed in the last chapter.

Other countries, both Allied and Axis, created propaganda with similar themes, all trying to discourage and depress the enemy soldiers. However, it has been determined since World War Two that the type of sexually explicit images that were being used in wartime propaganda increased, rather than decreased morale. Rather than feeling hopeless when they saw images of their wives and girlfriends being seduced by other men, this bolstered soldiers' enthusiasm for ending the war quickly and successfully.

The Holocaust, Part 1: The Targets

The Holocaust is by far the most famous part of World War Two. The word comes from the Greek words *"holos"* and *"kauston,"* meaning "everything burnt." If you don't know anything about the Battle of Stalingrad, the Allied and Axis powers, or even the War in the Pacific, you still know about the Holocaust: Hitler's massive scheme to exterminate anyone who he saw as "undesirable."

The biggest group of people targeted by the Holocaust was the Jewish population of Europe. Jewish people have been persecuted all throughout history, mostly for religious reasons, but Hitler had a new technique: race.

In the early 20th century, an idea called "eugenics" became popular. Eugenics was the idea that humanity could be systematically improved by encouraging people with "good genes" to have more children and people with "bad genes" to have fewer. In its early days, eugenics was instrumental in improving sexual education and access to birth control, and almost everyone supported it. However, Hitler decided to take it a step further by actually killing off the people with what he considered "bad genes." These included Jewish people, Romani people, gay men and lesbians, and people with mental or physical disabilities or chronic illnesses.

They also targeted communists and the Nazis' political opponents, so even if you happened to look like the Nazi ideal, you still weren't safe.

The Holocaust, Part 2: The Technique

The Nazis didn't just pick a day where they went out and gunned down all the "undesirables" in the street. The seeds of the Holocaust were sown long before the war, and each step of the process was only a small escalation from the one before it.

First, the Nazis began to capitalize on hatred that was already embedded in the culture. Jewish people, gay men and lesbians, disabled people, and Romani people (or "gypsies") had been targets of hatred for centuries, so it wasn't hard to stir up sentiment against them. The Nazis focussed on Jewish people because a significant number of them were well-off in comparison to Germany as a whole. Nazi propaganda claimed that it was the Jewish population's fault that so many Germans were living in poverty, even though we know it was because of the terms of the Treaty of Versailles, not some kind of Jewish conspiracy. They encouraged people to distrust, hate, and fear their neighbours.

They passed laws that limited human rights for Jewish citizens. These were called the Nuremberg Laws, and they prevented Jewish people from going to German schools, using sporting facilities, or even running businesses. It also required them to wear the famous yellow Star of David badges that marked them as Jews.

Then, Nazis started encouraging Aryan (white, non-Jewish, non-Romani, and otherwise "desirable") Germans to commit violence against their Jewish neighbours. They broke shop windows, stole property, and got into street brawls. One night of attacks was so bad that it became known as the Night of Broken Glass or *Kristallnacht*.

In 1941, after the war had broken out, the army started forming mobile killing units called *Einsatzgruppen* that shot Jewish and Romani people and dumped the bodies in mass graves. But this wasn't efficient enough for Hitler, so he ordered the construction of death camps where the Nazis could kill thousands of "undesirables" in minutes.

Concentration Camps

"Work camps" and prisoner-of-war camps weren't anything new in World War Two. They had been used all over Europe for centuries. Even during World War Two, the United States and Canada had their own "internment camps" where they imprisoned people from enemy countries. But the Nazis changed things in two important ways.

Firstly, the people put in the camps weren't enemy soldiers, they hadn't been convicted of any crimes, and they weren't prisoners of war. They were just normal German and Polish civilians. And secondly, while other camps were meant to contain their prisoners—and yes, conditions were bad and plenty of people died in them—the Nazi camps were made for the express purpose of killing as many people as possible.

Some prisoners were stripped naked and directed into rooms that were disguised as group showers, which were then filled with poison gas. Others were given back-breaking labour, like splitting rocks, to no end except to suffer. Still others became the subjects of gruesome medical experiments. Dead bodies were incinerated in giant ovens.

Outside of the concentration camps, people had a vague idea that people were going into these camps and not coming back, but no one knew the sheer scale of the death and destruction that was happening in them. It wasn't until 1944, when Allied troops finally took control of Poland and Germany that they started to discover the camps and free the prisoners.

The White Rose

Not everyone in Germany was on board with the Nazis. In fact, many of them strongly opposed it. The White Rose (or *die Weiße Rose* in German) was a resistance group centred in Munich in 1942 and 1943. They distributed leaflets and create anti-Nazi graffiti to try to break down the Nazi propaganda machine.

The leaflets talked about the war crimes the Nazis were committing, exposed the mass murder of Jewish citizens, and encouraged people to take a stand against the Nazi party. They also reached out to other resistance groups to share information.

The White Rose was active with students, starting at the University of Munich and spreading across the cities of Ulm and Stuutgart. The Catholic Church was also involved, and the Bishop August von Galen wrote a sermon against the Nazi regime that informed the population of the Concentration Camps and eugenic policies that the Nazis were using to "protect the German gene pool." Before this, most people in Germany didn't have a very strong understanding of what exactly was happening to their Jewish neighbours, which made it much harder to rally support against the Nazis.

A young woman named Sophie Scholl got permission to reprint the sermon and distribute it at her university. She, her brother, their professors, and their group of friends continued to distribute information like this until they were all arrested by the Gestapo in 1943 and found guilty of treason.

Operation Valkyrie

Operation Valkyrie, also known as the 20 July Plot, was a plan by Claus von Stauffenberg and a group of other unsatisfied Nazis to assassinate Adolf Hitler.

Stauffenberg and his co-conspirators had shared Hitler's ideology from the beginning, but by 1944, when Operation Valkyrie took place, it was obvious that Hitler was mad with power and that nothing was going to end well for Germany. Stauffenberg wanted to seize control of Germany and immediately make peace with the Allied powers. They were worried that when Germany inevitably fell to the Allies, they would think that all Germans were like Hitler and not hesitate to carry out mass executions or imprisonments.

The plan was to kill Hitler at a meeting in the *Wolfsschanze* conference room with a bomb hidden in a briefcase. Stauffenberg placed the bomb under the table at a conference near where Hitler was sitting and then received a planned phone call and left the room.

Unfortunately for Stauffenberg, a colonel who was in attendance pushed the suitcase out of the way behind the leg of the conference table, and when it exploded, it killed four people, wounded more than twenty, and left Hitler with only a singed uniform and a perforated eardrum.

Japan's Motivation

Okay, so now we know what was happening in Germany. The Nazis leveraged political dissatisfaction and hundreds of years of persecution towards killing off anyone they didn't think fit the mould of the "perfect German." But what about Japan?

Japan didn't care about the Jews. There were some Jewish people living in Japan, and they weren't exactly treated well (no one who wasn't Japanese was), but they weren't any worse off than Jews living in America, Britain, or the Soviet Union. So, if they didn't share the racial politics that made up the backbone of the Nazi party, why did Japan decide to side with the Nazis?

To put it simply, Japan was afraid of becoming irrelevant. In the nineteenth century, their neighbour, China, had gone from being a great power to being a fractured, crime-ridden, politically helpless state under the thumb of the British empire, and was not taken seriously by anyone.

Up until the 1850s, Japan had been an isolationist country, trying to stay out of the politics of the rest of the world. However, in the '50s, they realized that if they wanted to survive as a country and not be broken down the way China was, they were going to have to go from *isolationism* to *expansionism*.

Expansionism is just what it sounds like: the desire of a nation to expand. Japanese expansionists wanted to exert power over the entire Pacific area. While they were doing this, they adopted a lot of western conventions that made them seem like a more "modern" and therefore formidable adversary. They also, like any major power, started signing a lot of treaties with other countries, and, just like any major power, they entered World War One and took part in dismantling Germany's empire by taking over all their Pacific colonial properties.

In between the wars, they started getting more ambitious, but most of Europe wasn't very interested in expansionism because they didn't want another World War. So, Japan started to smooth things over with the one European country that *was* interested in expansionism—Germany.

For a while, Germany and Japan became uneasy allies, sharing certain ideals but unwilling to really work together. It wasn't until the outbreak of the war that they became official allies, basically operating under the old maxim "the enemy of an enemy is a friend."

Yamato

The world's biggest battleship was constructed in Japan between 1937 and 1940. It was a top-secret project carried out right in front of the American embassy. The only harbour big enough to carry out the project in was the Tokyo Harbour, which also happened to be where the Americans had their foreign embassy. Even though Japan and the United States were not at war yet, tensions were high, and the Japanese government knew that America wouldn't like them building such a massive battle ship.

The project for building Yamato was carried out in total secrecy. Screens and canopies were erected around the building site, the dock was lowered, and giant, powerful cranes were built on it to lift up the parts for the ship.

In 1940, when the ship was ready to be launched, the Japanese government developed the perfect scheme for making sure the Americans wouldn't see it. They declared a city-wide blackout. Claiming it was an air raid drill (a reasonable claim, seeing as air raids were an increasingly popular form of warfare), every building in the city was required to turn off their lights and paint their windows black. Of course, the American embassy did, giving the Japanese the chance to launch the Yamato.

Kamikaze

Another famous feature of World War Two was the Japanese technique of *kamikaze*, which has been translated as "divine wind." It was the word for the typhoons that killed Mongolian invaders of Japan in 1274, but now, it has entered the public consciousness as the name for pilots who carried out suicide attacks. It is also sometimes used to refer to other Japanese "suicide missions," like ones in submarines and speedboats.

In Japanese, the formal name for these attackers was *tokubetsu kōgeki tai*, which means "special attack unit." The word *kamikaze* was only used in informal press releases in Japan, but it caught the world's attention. In the modern world, a "kamikaze mission" is slang for any kind of activity that is dangerous to the point of practically being suicide.

Kamikaze aircraft were like a combination of an airplane and a missile—a giant airborne explosive, but one that had to be guided by an actual living human. Of course, practically everyone who flew a kamikaze aircraft died in the explosion when it hit its target, but it was meant to be more accurate (and able to carry more explosives) than a traditional attack, so it was seen as worth the loss of life.

Sadly for these unfortunate pilots, only 11% of all kamikaze attacks were successful. Even though the planes were easier to guide than a traditional missile, they were still very hard to navigate, and most missed their mark.

Bushido

In western culture, there is a major taboo against suicide. This is different from Japanese culture, where traditionally it was seen as a preferable option to a painful, gory, or humiliating death at the hands of an enemy. This comes from the tradition of *bushido*, which means "the way of the Samurai," and describes the proper way for a warrior to behave.

The concept of *bushido* is similar to the western idea of chivalry: a code of honour and morality for soldiers that regular people are also supposed to look up to. However, while the concept was probably *around* in earlier texts, *bushido* didn't become codified until the Renaissance. The word *bushido* didn't appear in Japanese until the seventeenth century and didn't become popular in common use until 1899. So, when World War Two broke out, the idea of *bushido* was pretty recently codified, although its roots went back much further.

Bushido was said by the writer and politician Nitobe Inazō to be made up of eight virtues: righteousness, heroic courage, benevolence, respect, integrity, honour, duty, and self-control. These virtues were leveraged by Japanese leaders to convince Japanese citizens to take part in the battles of World War Two.

Through indoctrination, propaganda, and some good old-fashioned arguing, leaders convinced their soldiers that the only way to properly express *bushido* was to do everything that they said, even if that meant laying down their lives. For this reason, Japanese soldiers were famous for their bravery in battle, apparently not fearing for their lives in the slightest, according to their enemies.

Life in Japan

Just like not every German was a Nazi, not every Japanese citizen agreed with their regime. Most people were just trying to live their lives. Leaders tried very hard to use the traditional Japanese cultural values of gratitude and repayment to convince citizens to want to do everything they could for their regime, but, of course, there was resistance. One Japanese soldier recounted an event where he went to retrieve bodies from a firebombing in Tokyo, and a woman shouted at him, "How do you feel about all these people? Can you look at them?"

Daily life for Japanese citizens was even more focussed than it was in European countries on "home front" efforts. Non-soldiers were still expected to do their part for the war effort by working in factories, making clothes for soldiers, giving up any luxury that could be contributed towards the war effort, and bolstering general support.

In 1943, children were sent to live in the countryside by the Japanese Ministry of Education, in a similar move to how British children were sent to the countryside during the Blitz. They wanted to evacuate children from cities to protect them from the bombings. Inns and Buddhist temples were used to house the children who couldn't go to relatives' homes. Everything had to be done to get them out of the way of the destruction.

The Last Soldier in World War Two

In the year 1974, 29 years after the end of World War Two, a Japanese soldier was discovered on Lubang, an island in the Pacific. This soldier, named Hiroo Onoda, had been an intelligence agent with the Japanese army, and in 1944, he had been sent to Lubang with the orders to do everything in his power to prevent it from falling into the hands of the allies. He was given explicit direction to never surrender and to never commit suicide.

In February 1945, American and Filipino forces landed on Lubang. The other soldiers on the island surrendered, but Onoda and three other soldiers escaped into the mountains. From their station, they engaged in guerilla warfare against the American forces even after they received a leaflet saying that the war had ended two months ago. They didn't believe that the leaflet was correct and thought it was a trap. Another leaflet was dropped on them at the end of the year, containing orders from the Japanese army to surrender, but only one of the four did. Of the remaining three, one died in 1954, and one in 1972, leaving only Onoda behind.

Finally, in February of 1974, a man named Norio Suzuki found Onoda and found out that he was not going to surrender until he received orders from an officer. Suzuki flew back to Japan and located Onoda's former commanding officer, who had since gotten a job selling books, and who finally gave Onoda the order to come out of hiding.

RANDOM FACTS

1. The popular orange soft drink *Fanta* was invented in Nazi Germany to replace American soft drinks, which they didn't want to import anymore. However, Germany didn't have a lot of supplies to make the drink and didn't want to import anything for it. They made the flavouring syrup out of whey (spoiled milk) and apple pomace (skin and seeds). The name came from the German word *Fantasie*, meaning "imagination" because they had to use their imagination when making it.

2. The swastika, which the Nazis used on their flag and uniforms, was actually an Indian symbol for the sun. This is why, if you pick up a first edition of Rudyard Kipling's famous book *The Jungle Book*, you may find that it has a swastika on the cover page.

3. Hitler personally designed the Nazi flag, choosing the colour red to represent the political idea of Nazism, white to represent white nationalism, and black to represent the German struggle.

4. Before developing the concentration camps, the Nazis considered getting rid of the Jews by shipping them to Madagascar, the way Britain

99

had tried to get rid of its criminals by shipping them to Australia.

5. Albert Speer, Adolf Hitler's chief architect, personally took moral responsibility for Nazi war crimes at the Nuremberg trials after the war, one of very few Nazis who accepted responsibility. The BBC made a documentary about him called *The Nazi who Said Sorry*.

6. Many medical experiments were carried out on prisoners in concentration camps. The Nazi regime was very interested in scientific discoveries, especially because they believed that a lot of science up until that point had been done by Jews and was therefore no good. The experiments were so gruesome and inhumane that the results from them are legally not allowed to be used today.

7. The most famous of those experiments were carried out by Dr. Joseph Mengele. He was interested in twins and used 3,000 pairs for his experiments, out of which only 200 survived. One experiment involved sewing two twins together to see if he could create conjoined twins.

8. The Nazis collected a lot of money and valuables from victims of the Holocaust. They put them into bank accounts under the false name "Max Heiliger."

9. In the 1920s, Germany was an unusually liberal country when it came to sexuality, and Berlin was the gay culture capital of the world. When the Nazi regime cracked down on homosexuality as "antisocial behaviour," they didn't have any trouble rounding up plenty of victims.

10. If you've ever travelled in Germany, especially in the Bavarian and Franconian regions, you may have stopped at a *Keller* to eat. "*Keller*" literally means "basement" (it's the origin of our word "cellar"), but it also refers to a specific type of restaurant, where beer, cheese, and cured meats are kept cool in caves in the hillsides. These caves ended up being useful to the Nazis for more than delicious refreshments. They used them as natural bomb shelters and even created munitions factories in the old underground breweries.

11. Before becoming leader of the SS, Heinrich Himmler, one of Hitler's right-hand men, was a chicken farmer.

12. One of the most famous quotes to come out of World War Two was a poem by Pastor Martin Niemöller, a German Lutheran pastor. He wrote, "First they came for the communists, and I did not speak out—because I was not a communist. Then they came for the trade unionists, and I did not speak out—because I was not a trade unionist. Then they came for the Jews, and I did not speak

out—because I was not a Jew. Then they came for me—and there was no one left to speak for me."

13. Hungary, one of the less powerful Axis nations, developed a series of laws called the "Jewish laws" that were similar to Germany's Nuremberg laws.

14. The famous Hungarian composer Béla Bartók loudly protested Hungary's involvement with Germany and made no secret of his disdain for Nazi politics.

15. In spite of Barók's open opposition to the Nazi regime, he remained a popular composer in Germany and was invited to perform at high-powered Nazi events. Why? Because all their best composers had been Jewish, and they no longer played Jewish music, so they had to take what they could get.

16. One of Japan's major problems, and the reason expansionist sentiment was so great, was because, as an island nation, they needed to import most of their goods. Annexing parts of China and Korea would have given them much better access to natural resources.

17. The Emperor of Japan is called the *Tennō*, which means "heavenly sovereign."

18. The Japanese attack on Pearl Harbour happened before Japan declared war on the United States,

making it a devastating surprise move. However, this wasn't actually the plan. Japan's admiral wanted to attack Pearl Harbour thirty minutes *after* declaring war and only got their early because the message declaring war took longer than planned to transcribe. Not that it would have made much difference. The plan was clearly to launch it as a surprise attack.

19. In Canada and the United States, thousands of Japanese-Canadian and Japanese-American citizens were rounded up and put in internment camps. The official reason for this was to protect them from racists in their own neighbourhood, but the actual reason was that the governments were worried that the Japanese in Canada and the US were more loyal to Japan than to the Allies and might spy on them or side with the Japanese during an attack.

20. Many of the children who were evacuated from Japanese cities in 1943 wrote letters and diaries about their experiences.

Test Yourself – Questions and Answers

1) What percentage of kamikaze attacks were successful?

   a. 84%
   b. 52%
   c. 11%

2) Who said the famous quote, "Where they have burned books, they will end in burning people"?

   a. Heinrich Heine
   b. Friedrich Nietzsche
   c. Martin Niemöller

3) Who said the famous quote, "First they came for the communists, and I did not speak out – because I was not a communist. Then they came for the trade unionists, and I did not speak out– because I was not a trade unionist. Then they came for the Jews, and I did not speak out– because I was not a Jew. Then they came for me– and there was no one left to speak for me."

   a. Heinrich Heine
   b. Friedrich Nietzsche
   c. Martin Niemöller

4) Which of these was not the name of an Operation in Germany?

   a. Operation Valkyrie
   b. Operation Husky

    c. Operation Hummingbird

5) What does *"bushido"* mean?

    a. "Honour and loyalty"
    b. "The way of the Samurai"
    c. "Divine wind"

Answers

1. c
2. a
3. c
4. b
5. b

CHAPTER FIVE

THE END OF THE WAR

After five years of fighting, and with the greatest death toll of any war in history (including unprecedented numbers of civilian deaths in both air raids and the Holocaust), World War Two was finally drawing to a close. Germany was buckling under the weight of attack after attack, and in 1945, the biggest man-made disaster in history was dropped from the sky right onto two of Japan's biggest cities, changing the course of both military and civilian history in the twentieth century.

World War Two was a difficult war to end because of how involved so many civilians were in it. This is one section where you're probably going to want to do a bit of extra research so you can really understand what was going on! But don't worry, we're going to cover all the most important parts, and learn a few weird details along the way.

The Casablanca Conference

We haven't talked much about the role of North Africa in World War Two, but if you've ever seen the classic noir film *Casablanca*, you might know that North Africa was a major hotbed for political action. North Africa had been mainly owned by the French, and when France surrendered to the Nazis, they thought that they'd be getting North Africa with it. However, Africa had different ideas, and the country of Morocco (Casablanca in particular) held out as loyal to the French until the end, even during Nazi occupation.

In January, 1943, several of the most significant allied leaders met at a hotel in Casablanca to discuss their war strategy. Franklin Delano Roosevelt was there, and so was Winston Churchill, as well as Charles de Gaulle and Henri Giraud, the representatives of the Free French Forces. The only Allied leader who neglected to show up was Joseph Stalin, who was busy with the Battle of Stalingrad in the Soviet Union.

It was at this convention that the leaders came up with their plans for proceeding against the Nazi forces. They discussed what their policies would be when it came to dealing with Axis powers. And they also formed the Casablanca Declaration, which described what they were planning on getting out of the war.

Borrowing a phrase from the American Civil War general Ulysses S. Grant, the Allied leaders agreed that they would accept nothing less than *unconditional surrender* from their enemies, and until that surrender was given, they would fight to the last man to achieve it. The only question was, how do you get such confident countries, ones that built entire ideologies on their innate, natural superiority, to agree to an unconditional surrender?

The Potsdam Declaration

The Potsdam Declaration's official name was "The Proclamation Defining Terms for Japanese Surrender," and it was written at the end of July in 1945 by the President of the United States, Harry S. Truman, the new Prime Minister of England Clement Attlee, and the Chairman of China, Chiang Kai-shek. They all got together and wrote the Potsdam Declaration at the Potsdam Conference, when they met to discuss the terms for Japan's surrender.

The Potsdam declaration demanded that Japan must eliminate all the leaders who had promoted the war, give up their territory to the allies, fully disarm their military, and allow all their leaders to stand trial for war crimes, for which they would be severely punished if found guilty.

It also offered freedom of speech and religion to the Japanese citizens and promised that Japan could maintain its industries. It also promised that Japanese people who weren't involved in war crimes would not be prosecuted on account of their nationality, and that the occupation of Japan would be as short-lived as possible.

Finally, it ended with the statement:

> We call upon the government of Japan to proclaim now the unconditional surrender of all Japanese armed forces, and to provide proper and adequate assurances of their good faith in such action. The alternative for Japan is prompt and utter destruction.

As far as the Allies were concerned, these were fair terms, so they didn't have any hesitation about telling the Japanese that, if they didn't accept the terms, they would face incredibly severe retribution. At the time, no one really knew how severe that retribution would be—not the Japanese, not the Allies, and not even the American scientists who ended up doling it out.

The Bomb, Part 1: What Is an Atom Bomb?

The atomic bombs that were dropped on Japan and ended World War Two are another one of those things that most people know about, even if they don't know anything about World War Two at all. But why were these bombs so much more important than any that got dropped on Germany, or Britain, or any other country during World War Two? What was it that made the atom bombs the decisive action in ending the war?

The bombs that got dropped on the two Japanese cities of Hiroshima and Nagasaki were a new type of weapon called *nuclear weapons*. They derived their power from splitting apart the nucleus of a single atom of hydrogen. This is called a "fission reaction."

If you know anything about chemistry, you know that an atom's nucleus, the core of the atom that makes up most of its weight and determines its chemical properties, is held together with incredibly strong forces. Splitting an atom had never been done before in history, but during World War Two, scientists discovered both how to split the atom and how to harness its incredible power for a bomb. The bomb was called the "atom bomb," or the "hydrogen bomb" or "H-bomb," since it used a hydrogen atom for the reaction.

Not only do fission reactions create a giant explosion, but they also create nuclear waste, the remains of the split atom. These remains are radioactive, meaning that they change without taking part in a chemical reaction. If a chemical changes without taking part in a chemical reaction, it is *unstable* and prone to creating unpredictable reactions with the other atoms around it. This leads to it reacting with and decaying living tissue, such as the bodies of people who are too close to it. This can cause birth defects, blood cell death, damage to the nervous system, and all sorts of cancer.

The Bomb, Part 2: Hiroshima

Over the course of World War Two, American scientists had been developing nuclear weapons, and on August 6, 1945, they were finally ready to use them. By this time, Germany had already surrendered to the Allies (they did this about three months earlier, on May 8th), but Japan was holding out. The Allied powers wanted an unconditional surrender, which Japan was simply not willing to give them.

They chose the city of Hiroshima as their first target because it was an industrial city with a lot of military units in the area, and it also contained the headquarters of the Second General Army, which was in charge of defending all of southern Japan. It was also the second-largest Japanese city, with about 350,000 citizens.

Just after midnight on August 6, a bomb was loaded into a plane called the *Enola Gay*. At 8:15 that morning, the bomb was dropped directly over a surgical clinic, 800 feet from the intended target, but the inaccuracy didn't matter. It destroyed a mile of land in an instant, and the firestorm cloud that resulted from the explosion reached its strongest intensity three hours later, with a thousand times the energy of the initial explosion. 30% of the population of Hiroshima were killed within those first few hours. 70,000 were injured. 90% of Hiroshima's doctors, and 93% of its nurses, were killed or injured, since they had been close to the site of the explosion. Only one doctor remained at their Red Cross Hospital.

Radar detectors outside the city were confused at the sudden loss of contact with Hiroshima. After all, only one bomb had been dropped.

The Bomb, Part 3: Nagasaki

Japan was reeling from the realization that they had been hit with a weapon unlike anything the world had ever seen before. No one knew how to handle the situation and panic was widespread as another Japanese city became a target.

Nagasaki was mainly used as a seaport, and, like Hiroshima, had a huge amount of industrial value for the United States. About 90% of Nagasaki's work force worked at the shipyards, arms works, and steel factories. However, up until August 9, it hadn't been firebombed much, because its compact size (only four square miles) and placement around a mountain range made it difficult to accurately locate on radar.

Early in the morning of August 9, the Japanese noticed two planes flying overhead but assumed that since they were only two, they were reconnaissance planes. At 11:01, a bomb was dropped right over a tennis court, three miles northwest of the planned target.

Although this bomb was even bigger and stronger than the Hiroshima bomb, its effects were contained by Nagasaki's natural geography, but it killed around 40,000 citizens and injured 60,000 more, even before the hundreds of thousands who would eventually suffer the effects of radiation poisoning from the bomb. A wind spread the fire along the valley.

The Japanese Surrender

After these two events, it was obvious to the Japanese that there was no winning. On August 15, 1945, less than a week after the second bomb was dropped on Nagasaki, Japan responded to the Allied call for an unconditional surrender. They forfeited all rights to make demands in the post-war negotiations.

They did try to get the Soviet Union, which had been a little more neutral towards Japan than the other Allies, to negotiate more favourable terms for them. However, the Soviet Union had no intentions of doing anything Japan said, and was, in fact, secretly plotting to conquer the Japanese holdings in Manchuria and Korea that had set off the war more than a decade earlier.

Japan had always promised to fight to the bitter end until every single soldier was dead. This was the official stance of the Japanese Supreme Council for the Direction of the War. However, after the two bombs, Emperor Hirohito himself intervened and demanded that the Supreme Council for the Direction of the War accept the Allies' terms of surrender. The loss of civilian life was far too great to risk again, and no one knew how many more bombs the Americans might have in store (in actual fact, it was zero, but the Americans weren't exactly broadcasting that fact).

In his address to the Japanese people, Emperor Hirohito said:

> After pondering deeply the general trends of the world and the actual conditions obtaining in our empire today, we have decided to effect a settlement of the present situation by resorting to an extraordinary measure.

> We have ordered our government to communicate to the governments of the United States, Great Britain, China, and the Soviet Union that our empire accepts the provisions of their joint declaration.

> To strive for the common prosperity and happiness of all nations as well as the security and well-being of our subjects is the solemn obligation which has been handed down by our imperial ancestors and which lies close to our heart.

> Indeed, we declared war on America and Britain

out of our sincere desire to ensure Japan's self-preservation and the stabilization of East Asia, it being far from our thought either to infringe upon the sovereignty of other nations or to embark upon territorial aggrandizement.

But now the war has lasted for nearly four years.

Followed by one of history's great understatements:

Despite the best that has been done by everyone—the gallant fighting of the military and naval forces, the diligence and assiduity of our servants of the state, and the devoted service of our one hundred million people—the war situation has developed not necessarily to Japan's advantage.

Volkssturm

Let's move back to the European theatre, where the situation was no less dramatic. The Nazis knew that things were falling apart. They had lost most of their best troops in battle on the Eastern Front, especially in the brutal siege at Stalingrad. Besides that, morale was at an all-time low, with more and more German citizens becoming disillusioned with the Nazi regime. Hitler was no longer the handsome, stylish man in Hugo Boss, surrounded by fawning crowds while making compelling speeches. Now, even to the most patriotic Germans, he was an increasingly dangerous madman who would send them to their deaths at any moment.

This reached its peak in October 1944, when a militia group called the *Volkssturm* was announced. This was part of the Propaganda Minister Joseph Goebbels' plan for total war, but he was the only person excited about it. The *Volkssturm* demanded that every man between the age of 16 and 60 (far outside the range that had been allowed to fight before) take up arms and fight to the death against any invading soldier. It didn't matter if you had been deemed unfit before or were too old or too young, or had recently been injured—all hands were on deck.

Unsurprisingly, the *Volkssturm* were poorly prepared, and it was another nail in the coffin for Nazi popularity. Thousands of men who should have been protected were sent to their deaths.

Liberating the Concentration Camps

The Nazis surrendered in the spring of 1945, but starting about a year earlier, in July 1944, the single biggest blow was dealt to the popular support of Hitler's regimes: The Allies found the concentration camps.

In July, 1944, Soviet troops found the Majdanek camp in Poland. The German soldiers attending the camp had not expected this and realized in a panic that they would be instantly convicted of war crimes (if not shot on the spot) if the death camps were exposed. They tried to demolish the camp as the Soviet troops approached, using the crematorium to incinerate the prisoners, but they couldn't knock down the gas chambers before the Soviets reached it.

The biggest concentration camp, Auschwitz, was liberated by the Soviets in January, 1945. The Nazis had tried to march the prisoners out of the camp, but six thousand were still there, along with warehouses full of prisoners' personal belongings.

The tiny proportion of prisoners who survived the concentration camps were starved, emaciated, disease-ridden, and bore unspeakable injuries from labour and medical experiments alike. Hundreds of the liberating soldiers reported symptoms of post-traumatic stress disorder in later years from the experience of seeing so many "living skeletons" and realizing what the Nazis had really been doing to their citizens for all this time.

The Morgenthau Plan

The Morgenthau Plan was a proposed strategy from the Allied powers to make it impossible for Germany to ever fight in another war. It would prevent them from developing an armaments industry, creating an army, or building up the industrial power necessary for modern warfare. It would also divide Germany into several smaller, less powerful pieces that would be controlled by various Allied countries, including the Soviet Union, France, and Poland.

It was recommended by Henry Morgenthau, the American Secretary of the Treasury, in 1944, in a memorandum called "Suggested Post-Surrender Program for Germany," in his book *Germany is our Problem*.

Many people, including leader of the Soviet Union Joseph Stalin and American president Franklin Delano Roosevelt, supported the plan. They saw it as a better version of the Treaty of Versailles, one that would truly stop Germany from rising up in rebellion as they had done in the 1930s. No one wanted to be too lenient on the Germans after their war crimes. Secretary of State Cordell Hull wanted the Germans to be "fed three times a day with soup from Army soup kitchens... [so] they will remember that experience the rest of their lives."

When this plan got out to the Germans, they were furious. They hadn't even lost the war yet, and already, the Americans were making plans to annex them! The Nazis ended up using this as propaganda fodder, convincing the worn-out German soldiers to fight on lest they fall victim to this plan.

Hitler's Suicide

On April 30, 1945, Hitler and his mistress (and wife for the past two days) Eva Braun committed suicide in a bunker under Berlin.

It had been clear for the past two years that the wheels were coming off the Nazi regime and that Hitler's plans for a German empire were not to be fulfilled. The crushing defeat at Stalingrad had decimated the German forces, and the Battle of Berlin was raging outside. It was a siege-style attack, with the Soviet army cutting off the German citizens inside from everything.

Hitler had created a bunker underneath Berlin that had its own water and electricity, and he and his right-hand men (and Eva Braun) withdrew into it. Reports described Hitler as increasingly unravelled, and if it hadn't been clear before that he was insane, it was now. However, he continued to give military orders in spite of the obvious inevitable defeat.

Forty hours before his suicide, he married Eva Braun in a small civil ceremony and appointed his Admiral Karl Donitz as head of state. He and Eva then poisoned themselves with cyanide capsules. Hitler shot himself in the head for good measure, and their bodies were cremated before the Soviet army reached the building. Eight days later, the German army surrendered unconditionally.

Victory in Europe Day

Victory in Europe Day, known as VE Day for short, is celebrated all over Europe on May 8. It marks the day of the Nazi's unconditional surrender. Soviet countries have traditionally celebrated it on May 9, and in the Ukraine, it is not listed as a public holiday but it is still observed as a day of Remembrance and Reconciliation.

In the United Kingdom, when victory over the Axis powers was announced on March 8, over one million people joined the public celebrations in the streets. These people included the princesses of England themselves, Elizabeth and Margaret! King George VI, his wife Queen Elizabeth, and Winston Churchill appeared on the Buckingham Palace balcony to wave to the cheering crowds.

It also happened to fall on the birthday of Harry Truman, the President of the United States. He described it as "his most enjoyable birthday."

It is observed officially in over fifteen countries, where it goes by a variety of names, like the Italian "Festa della Liberazione" (Liberation Festival) and the Slovakian "Deň víťazstva nad fašizmom" (Victory over Fascism Day).

Victory over Japan Day

In a similar vein, Victory over Japan day is celebrated on August 15 in Britain, and September 2 in the

United States. Britain celebrates it on the date of Japan's announcement of surrender, and the United States on the date when the official surrender document was signed.

Celebrations of Japan's surrender were even more dramatic than the ones that had been celebrated over Germany a few months earlier. Allied soldiers danced a conga line in London, while the American soldiers in Berlin raised a city-wide chant of "It's over in the Pacific!"

However, the way in which the war in the Pacific had been won was a little more concerning than Germany's surrender had been. People were happy that the war was over, but they were also worried about the implications that the atomic bomb was going to have for world politics, and they were right to be. Germany was glad that the bomb wasn't going to be used on them, but the Soviet Union was a little more hesitant, and the government refused to make an official statement about the bomb. As it turned out, the Soviet Union had plans to become a nuclear superpower, and the strain between the United States and the Soviet Union was one that was going to colour the next two decades of politics and culture.

However, in spite of the palpable strain, *Life* magazine described the celebration "as if joy had been rationed and saved up for the three years, eight months, and seven days since Sunday, Dec. 7, 1941."

The Nuremberg Trials

The Nuremberg Trials, which took place from 1945 to 1946, were a series of twenty-two hearings that tried major Nazi figures for war crimes and crimes against humanity.

The trials took place in Nuremberg (or *Nürnberg*), which had been the seat of the Nazi regime. They justified this by claiming that it had been the seat of the Holy Roman Empire. Seven years earlier, it had been in Nuremberg that Hitler held the famous Nuremberg Rallies where the Nazis held a series of sporting and cultural events to show off their perceived superiority, and where Hitler gave some of his most memorable speeches. Now, the leaders were defeated and forced to face payment for their crimes.

Of course, Hitler, the leader who most deserved the punishment, was not there to be tried. Without his presence, it was difficult to know how to assign blame. Other significant Nazis, like Heinrich Himmler and Joseph Goebbels, had also committed suicide to avoid trial, and others fled to Argentina to avoid being captured.

All those tried were tested for their intelligence (most scored unusually high and their psychiatric stability to ensure that they were fit to stand trial. Then, over the course of almost a year, the criminals were systematically examined. Films of the concentration camps were submitted as evidence, and witnesses testified that they had been given orders to "exterminate" as many people as they could. They described the eugenic plan for removing everyone "undesirable" from the gene pool—the "Final Solution." One Nazi, Otto Ohlendorf, admitted—without emotion—that he had murdered 90,000 Jewish people.

Of the twenty-two tried Nazis, twelve were sentenced to death.

The Banality of Evil

In 1960, Adolf Eichmann, who had escaped from Germany and into Argentina, was captured and put on trial in Jerusalem. A German Jewish woman named Hannah Arendt reported on his trial for *The New Yorker* and discovered some disturbing features of his defence, which she wrote about in her book *Eichmann in Jerusalem: A Report on the Banality of Evil*.

Over the course of the Nuremberg Trials, but most famously in Eichmann's trial, one defence came up over and over: the people on trial were "just following orders." They explained, sometimes desperately, sometimes matter-of-factly, that if they hadn't participated in running the concentration camps and the secret police, they would have been breaking the law, morally wrong and punishable by death. Eichmann wrote, "He did his *duty*... he not only obeyed *orders,* he also obeyed the *law."*

Eichmann claimed that he followed Immanuel Kant's theory of the categorical imperative: "act only according to that maxim where you can, at the same time, will that it should become a universal law." But instead of understanding this as a "treat others how you want to be treated" moral, Eichmann understood it as following the laws of the world, which, for Eichmann, meant following the orders of his leader.

Arendt also accused Eichmann of being unable to think for himself, not particularly intelligent, and a "joiner." In other words, she claimed, it was not some grand evil scheme that made him commit the terrible crimes that characterized his life, but instead, he was attracted to the feelings of security and camaraderie that the Nazi army instilled in him, and was not intelligent enough to question their underlying philosophies.

Arendt's phrase, "the banality of evil," describes this: that the people who carried out crimes were not insane or evil, but average people who were driven by completely unexceptional concerns, like wanting to fit in, and wanting to have a steady career. The hatred and anti-Semitism that Eichmann ended up acting on, according to Arendt, were just by-products of his normal, "banal" interests.

Just Following Orders

Stanley Milgram, a professor of psychology at Yale University, didn't think that "the banality of evil," that people commit atrocities when they are told to, was a very good excuse. In his opinion, the only way to commit so many crimes with so little emotional response was to be a sociopath. But did that mean that everyone in Germany had been a sociopath for an entire decade?

So Milgram devised an experiment to see what, exactly, people would do when they were "just following orders." He developed an experiment, known today as the Milgram experiment, to test whether people really would be willing to do terrible things if an authority told them to.

First, for the experiment, Milgram hired a group of actors who would sit in a room with a microphone. Then, he collected some enthusiastic psychology students, whom he dressed in professional medical uniforms. Finally, he put out a call for participants, claiming that the psychology department was doing a study on the effect of physical pain on memory.

He put the participants and the medical students in one room and the actors in the other with a microphone so they could hear each other but not see each other. The students would explain to the participants that they were going to ask the actors (who they called "learners") a series of memory questions, and if the "learners" got them wrong, the participants (who they called "teachers") had to give them an electric shock. The shocks were delivered by a piece of scary-looking machinery, with a dial that indicated a range of strengths and a button to deliver the shocks. Every time the "learner" got an answer wrong, the students explained, the "teacher" was to increase the voltage by 15 volts.

The experiment began with the "teachers" pressing the shock button as instructed by the students. These buttons didn't really do anything, but in the other room, the "learners" would yelp, scream, and complain. As the voltage went up higher and higher, the screaming became more intense.

Most "teachers" paused at some point, asking if they should stop or check on the "learners," but the students assured them that they would not be held responsible for any injury… and they continued. If the "teachers" asked to stop, they were given four vocal prods, in this order:

"Please continue."

"The experiment requires that you continue."

"It is absolutely essential that you continue."

"You have no other choice. You *must* go on."

Only if the "teacher" still objected after all four

statements was he allowed to go. If he didn't, he had to deliver a lethal "shock" of 450 volts three times, after which the "learner" would go quiet.

What Milgram learned from this experiment was shocking and disturbing: although the "teachers" expressed stress, fear, and emotional pain at what they were doing, 65% of all these normal people were willing to (they believed) kill another human when they were being ordered to by someone in a uniform.

RANDOM FACTS

1. The old men in the *Volkssturm* weren't beyond poking fun at their absurd situation. They joked, "Why is the *Volkssturm* Germany's most precious resource? Because its members have silver in their hair, gold in their mouths, and lead in their bones."

2. The photography aircraft that followed the *Enola Gay* to document the destruction in Hiroshima didn't have a name when it was launched, but it was later named *Necessary Evil*.

3. Lieutenant General James H. Doolittle warned Japan, after the two atomic bombs were dropped, that they would "eventually be a nation without cities—a nomadic people."

4. President Truman said of the atomic bomb project that the United States had "spent two billion dollars on the greatest scientific gamble in history—and won."

5. Right before the bombing of Nagasaki, a letter was dropped by the American planes to a professor at the University of Tokyo, begging him to tell people about the dangers associated with atomic bombs.

6. The nuclear physicist Niels Bohr was being forced

to work for the Germans in occupied Denmark when resistance fighters gave him the opportunity to escape, along with a bottle of "heavy water" — water that contains the hydrogen atoms used for nuclear reactors. When he arrived in England, it was revealed that his "heavy water" was, in fact, beer.

7. The Nazi party generally resisted investing money in nuclear development because most of the pioneering nuclear physicists had happened to be Jewish. They treated it with intense suspicion, as a "Jew science."

8. The declaration of Japanese surrender, given by Emperor Hirohito on August 15, 1945, was delivered in classical Japanese, and was the first time most Japanese citizens had ever heard their emperor's voice.

9. In spite of the atrocities that Jewish people experienced in the Nazi concentration camps, reported rates of post-traumatic stress disorder in the Jewish community have remained relatively low. Psychologists speculate that this is because most Jewish people have very strong ties to a tight-knit community, which helps them successfully cope with trauma.

10. Anne Frank, the teenage girl whose diary is one of the most famous accounts of life during the

Holocaust, died of typhus in the Bergen-Belsen concentration camp less than two months before the camp was liberated by the British, although the exact dates are unknown.

11. Some war scholars estimate that if just 1% of the bombs that the Allies dropped on German industries had been dropped on their power plants instead, the fragile German power grid would have collapsed, and the war could have been won much faster.

12. Hitler and Eva Braun poisoned their dogs with the same cyanide capsules that they used to commit suicide.

13. Remember Unity Mitford, the British woman who had an affair with Hitler? Allegedly, when Hitler committed suicide in 1945, the daughter of the family she was staying with told her, "I'm sorry your boyfriend died."

14. After Hitler's cremation, his ashes were moved repeatedly to avoid becoming the focal point for a shrine or any sort of Nazi adoration.

15. World War Two was the first war where film evidence was used to convict war criminals. The novelty and quantity of the footage of Nazi Germany has contributed to the Holocaust being the best-remembered genocide in history, although contemporaneous dictators like Stalin

had similarly high body counts.

16. The Nuremberg Trials were the first trials in history to try war criminals with judges from four different countries. It set the stage for today's international law trials.

17. The Nuremberg Trials were also the first-ever trials to convict anyone of the offence "crimes against humanity," meaning atrocities so severe that they markedly damaged the entire human race.

18. One more first for the Nuremberg Trials: the prosecution against the Nazi officials was the first to coin the term "genocide" for the systematic murder of a group of people based on a shared characteristic, like race.

19. For decades after the end of World War Two, people in America were on the lookout for ex-Nazis and Nazi sympathizers in their own towns, until it became more fashionable to try to hunt down communists instead.

20. Of all the participants in the Milgram experiment, 84% said that they were happy to have taken part. They said that the experiment made them braver and more conscious of their own role in speaking out for others.

Test Yourself – Questions and Answers

1) Which city was not targeted by atom bombs?

   a. Tokyo
   b. Hiroshima
   c. Nagasaki

2) Who surrendered first?

   a. Japan
   b. Germany
   c. They surrendered at the same time

3) What were the *Volkssturm*?

   a. German resistance fighters
   b. Troops made up of people who had not been drafted before
   c. Hitler's personal bodyguards

4) Which of these did *not* happen for the first time at the Nuremberg Trials?

   a. Someone was convicted of "crimes against humanity"
   b. The term "genocide" was used
   c. A war criminal personally presented his own defence

5) What did the Milgram experiment test?

   a. People's ability to remember information while being subjected to electrical shocks

b. People's tendency to follow orders in spite of their personal moral objections
c. The speed at which a person in a position of power turns to violence

Answers

1. a
2. b
3. b
4. c
5. b

CHAPTER SIX

WORLD WAR TWO IN MEDIA AND CULTURE

It's almost impossible to imagine a world today without World War Two. What would it look like? Well, we wouldn't have had the nuclear age or the Cold War. We probably wouldn't have sent a man to the moon. Our movie villains wouldn't wear Hugo Boss-inspired uniforms, duck-step in formation, or talk about "exterminating" the enemy. In fact, the world of popular media would be totally unrecognizable.

In this chapter, we're going to look at the fallout from World War Two and how it affected people once peace had been re-established. We'll see how some different people reacted to the war, from people who wanted nice, normal families, to people who wanted to throw the whole world away.

We're also going to take a look at some famous books and movies that were made during or about World War Two, because watching movies is always the most fun way to understand history!

Back to Normal in the '50s

After five years of wholesale slaughter, tight rationing, and women working in factories while men died on the battlefields, most people in the 1950s were eager to return to a "simpler" way of life. Men were providers who went to a 9-to-5 job, while women took care of the house and children. It was a return to gender norms that hadn't been this strict since the 1850s. This was the time when the "nuclear family" became popular, and the ideal became "a mother, a father, and two-and-a-half children"—the two-and-a-half children referring to the statistically average number of children in an American household.

A high premium was also placed on having material things after the rationing of World War Two. People wanted fancy cars, beautiful houses, and lots of electronic gadgets, like TVs and microwaves. In the broad strokes, it was a time of prosperity.

However, there were cracks in the façade, and peace came at a cost. Rigid conformity was encouraged, and there were strict social sanctions for failing to meet expectations. Many men who had been in the war had difficulty adapting to peacetime norms, and the metaphorical (as well as literal) fallout from the nuclear bombings was casting a long shadow over the former Allied nations.

The Beat Generation

The strict notions of conformity that characterized the 1950s did not look kindly upon things like experimental art, bohemian lifestyles, homosexuality, or drug use. The Beat Generation were a group of young people in the 1950s who decided to take up everything that the general culture of the 1950s was against and bear it with pride.

These young people were mainly men, mainly from relatively affluent families, who felt that they were being intellectually underserved by the culture of the 1950s. Probably most famous was Allen Ginsberg, the "visionary angel" who wrote "Howl," one of the most famous poems of the century. He had grown up in a Jewish family in New Jersey, in a family ravaged by cultural stress as well as mental illness. His battle cry, "I saw the best minds of my generation destroyed by madness," tapped into the rage that had been left behind by the war but that no one dared speak about.

The "establishment" (that is, non-Beat) art of the 1950s was far, far bleaker than Ginsberg's ode to those "destroyed by madness," and the Beats brought strong emotion, joy, and anger to an artistic scene that was full of solipsism and depression. However, their outbursts met with censure from the general public, who accused them of moral degeneracy and dangerous criminality.

PTSD

Most of the Beat poets hadn't been in the war in person, although they had seen older friends and family members slaughtered in it. For the men who had been on the front lines, the emotional response associated with coming back to safety and peacetime was even more severe.

Many of the men who returned from the war had symptoms of what we now call post-traumatic stress disorder, although then, it was known as "shell shock" or "battle fatigue." Post-traumatic stress disorder (PTSD for short) is characterized by persistent, intense memories of traumatic events and difficulty integrating into a new, non-traumatic environment.

At the time (and even today), resources for war veterans with PTSD were very limited. No one knew exactly how to deal with this problem or how they could help the men who were suffering from it. Besides that, since there was no real knowledge about the problem, most of the men suffering from it felt that what they were feeling was weakness or cowardice and were unwilling to tell anyone about it.

Even the men who didn't exhibit symptoms of PTSD had difficulty re-integrating into peaceful America. In the army, they had been surrounded by other men, mostly of similar backgrounds, and united by an ideological framework. Once they got back home, many of them complained that they didn't have any feelings of camaraderie anymore. Going back to working a 9-5 job where they didn't have emotional connections to anyone around them left many men feeling disillusioned, alienated, and alone.

Nuclear Fallout

In addition to the strain of conformity and the post-traumatic stress that many ex-soldiers experienced, the new threat of nuclear war hung heavily over the world. The Soviet Union had never been quite perfectly aligned with the goals of the other Allied countries during World War Two, and in the wake of the war, it became increasingly clear that the only political point they had ever had in common with the United States was that they didn't like the Nazis. Furthermore, it was becoming clear that, while no one *wanted* another war, another one might not be far away.

The Americans had proven they had access to nuclear technology that could wipe out entire cities in the blink of an eye and that the technology would only become more effective with time. At the same time, the Soviet Union was developing their own nuclear program.

In 1947, American President Harry S. Truman made a promise that the United States would help any country that was being "threatened" by the Soviet

Union's expansionist tactics. Any country that was in the Soviet sphere of influence, or that held similar political doctrines (read: communism) was of interest to the United States. They also indicated—although didn't exactly state outright— that if they needed to, they wouldn't hesitate to use nuclear weapons against the Soviet Union.

What do you get when two countries with world-ending weapons decide that they're enemies? Decades of intense anxiety, fear of nuclear warfare at any moment, and the doctrine of "mutually assured destruction."

Post-War Women

During World War Two, women took on much more significant roles in the workforce than they had at any time before, even during World War One (which was already a huge stride forward!). More and more, women were expecting—in fact, *demanding*—that the men around them take them seriously as equals.

In 1948, President Harry Truman signed the Women's Armed Services Integration Act, which allowed women to serve in the military. Previously, they had been allowed to work as nurses, in munition factories, and do work on the home front like making uniforms for soldiers, but their roles in actually fighting were extremely limited.

Truman's signature of the WASI Act prompted the formation of the Women in the Air Force program, or WAF, which allowed female pilots to join the Air Force Reserves, and also trained non-pilot women to do clerical and medical work for the Air Force.

While lots of women were interested in these programs, there was also a lot of pushback. Men complained that the war was over and women shouldn't be getting involved in military activities, but instead should stay home and take care of families. Slander campaigns alleged that women in the military were sexually promiscuous, depraved, and generally immoral, citing trumped-up charges of women in uniform getting into street fights as examples of their "unfeminine" behaviour.

Although a handful of women stuck it out and stayed with the Army and Air Force, the vast majority folded back into the highly traditional family roles that were being demanded of them. For over a decade, that was the status quo, and only in the 1960s did second-wave feminism emerge to challenge that mentality. By the 1960s, most people no longer vividly remembered what it was like to be forced to live in an "incomplete" household, and so the threat of a household not adhering perfectly to the standards of the "nuclear family" was holding less and less weight.

World War Two on the Silver Screen

World War Two had a ripple effect on culture for decades (one that is still going on today and will probably go on for hundreds of years more), but one of its most obvious effects is the one that it's had on mass media. World War Two was only the second major war since the invention of film in the 1890s, and it was the first one where film was a big part of both propaganda and news about the war. The abundance of news footage made it very easy for filmmakers since then to capture World War Two on the screen.

There have been hundreds of films about World War Two—about the Holocaust, the Nazis, the American soldiers, the French Resistance, Pearl Harbour, D-Day, the atomic bombs, and virtually any other aspect of the War you could imagine—not to mention dozens of television serials and a virtually uncountable number of documentaries.

We couldn't possibly look at every single media portrayal of World War Two, but there are some stories that just keep coming back, so read on to learn more about some of the many, many movies made about World War Two!

German Art Films

If you're into film, you've probably watched a lot of German movies from the period between World War

One and the rise of the Nazi party in the 1930s. And if you're not into film, you probably haven't seen any of them, but you might still be familiar with names like *Dr. Caligari* and *Nosferatu*. Before World War Two, Germany had a great art cinema scene, with films like *The Cabinet of Dr. Caligari* and the works of Fritz Lang. Most movies were either horror or historical fiction, or a combination of both.

A recurring theme in these movies was finding a balance between "tyranny and chaos" (as the critic Siegfried Kracauer described in his book *From Caligari to Hitler*). German filmmakers got slammed by the Nazi regime (it was pretty hard to make a movie that the Nazis wouldn't object to, unless you were making them specifically for the party, under careful observation and instruction), but the art film scene still reflected people's views about politics, which shaped the war.

There was a lot of tension about authority. Who should have it? What happens when it's misused? And what happens when no one has authority? What happens when we're only slaves to ourselves? Is that just as bad as a bad authority? Is it even worse? These were questions that the Nazi party claimed to have answers to.

Kracauer argued that, because films take a lot of people to make and produce, films (even non-political or "escapist" ones) revealed underlying patterns in people's ideas about the world. If we look at the films from a time period, we can start to guess what the people at that time were thinking about. What does that mean for us today, when we're so obsessed with putting World War Two on film over and over again?

Saving Private Ryan, *Dunkirk*, and Other Action Epics

When it comes to American portrayals of World War Two, most films that focus on the American soldiers (rather than the Holocaust) are epic action dramas based on real battles and people. Two of the biggest examples of this type of film are 1998's classic *Saving Private Ryan*, directed by Steven Spielberg, and 2017's *Dunkirk*, directed by Christopher Nolan. Both of these movies were directed by world-famous directors, had star-studded casts, and featured massive, gory action scenes based on real-life battles.

Saving Private Ryan was loosely based on the real-life story of Edward Niland, who was presumed dead in 1944, but had actually been captured and kept in a Japanese prisoner of war camp for a year. In *Saving Private Ryan*, a man named James Ryan is found missing in action after the D-Day battle, and the War Department takes the initiative to go find Ryan because his three brothers were already killed in the war. It focusses on the bonds that formed between soldiers on the front, especially with Ryan's line about his fellow soldiers being "the only brothers [he has] left." It's also famous for its enormous cinematic portrayal of the Invasion of Normandy (D-Day), which was shot on the coast of Ireland and hired actual soldiers and amputees to act as extras. It was named the "best battle scene of all time" by *Empire* magazine.

Similar, but different, was Christopher Nolan's recent film *Dunkirk*, which has been named one of the best films of the 21st century by *IndieWire* magazine. Unlike *Saving Private Ryan*, *Dunkirk*'s characters are very simple, and there isn't much dialogue between them. Instead, the focus is the amazing, tension-building score and the shuddering action scenes of explosions and shootings. This was all part of Christopher Nolan's plan to capture the emptiness and brutality of World War Two. The *Hollywood Reporter* called it "impressionist" because it captured the "feel" of war, rather than telling a regular story.

So, these movies have two wildly different approaches to telling the stories of World War Two, with *Saving Private Ryan* being about the people and humanity who got caught up in fighting, while *Dunkirk* is about the cold brutality of war. But both of them have a very similar purpose: to get the audience's heart racing and to (hopefully) fill them with a sense of tragic heroism.

Other movies in this vein include Michael Bay's *Pearl*

Harbour, Quentin Tarantino's *Inglourious Basterds*, and Spike Lee's *Miracle at St. Anna*. World War Two is always a popular topic for high-powered movie producers!

The Influence

While there's no shortage of movies explicitly about World War Two, there are even more that use the imagery and "story" of the war to punch up an unrelated film.

For example, here's a film you've probably seen: Disney's *The Lion King*. It was the highest-grossing animated movie of all time when it came out in 1994, and it tells the story of a lion cub whose father, the king of the Pride Lands, is killed by his evil, scheming brother, Scar.

How do we know that Scar is evil? Well, for one thing, he kills his brother. But even before that, we get to see a dramatic musical number where Scar relates his plans while pontificating on a high podium, overlooking a sea of his underlings (hyenas) marching in tight formation. You might not have noticed it as a kid, but if you look back at it now, it'll be hard not to see how much the Disney animators were inspired by the famous footage of Hitler speaking at the Nuremberg rallies when they created that scene.

Other directors get even more explicit, like Richard

Loncraine, in his version of Shakespeare's play *Richard III* that stars Sir Patrick Stewart (of *Star Trek* and *X-Men* fame). From Patrick Stewart's one-armed salute, to the red banners with a white circle and a black symbol, everything about the character Richard III's tyrannical government mirrors the Nazi party.

Both Loncraine and Disney knew that making your audience think about Nazis is the fastest way to get them to think that your villain is evil!

Nazisploitation: *Salon Kitty* and its Imitators

Most of the time, making your audience think about Nazis is a quick way to convey that your villain is evil. But sometimes you get movies that take a... different approach to Nazi imagery.

Among the more bizarre sub-genres of World War Two-related films is the "Nazisploitation" genre, which uses hypersexualized imagery, usually combined with sadomasochistic themes and graphic sex and violence, to create either moderately or outright pornographic representations of World War Two.

Remember the Salon Kitty, the Nazi brothel in Berlin that we talked about in Chapter Four? There was a movie about it! In 1976, the Italian film director Tinto Brass directed *Salon Kitty* as an erotic thriller about prostitutes spying on the customers at their brothel. It was an Italian/France/German co-production, and in its original cut, it had heavy political themes, which were lightened for its United States release, where it was marketed as a straight-up "exploitation" sex movie.

There was no shortage of imitators, most of which dropped the political themes and "based on a true story" context, replacing it with even more overblown S&M scenes and women in short-skirted or low-cut variations on Stormtrooper uniforms.

To say the least, it is a controversial genre.

The Diary of Anne Frank

The Diary of Anne Frank, also published as *Diary of a Young Girl*, is one of history's most famous diaries. Anne Frank was a German girl raised in the Netherlands, who, at the age of 13, went into hiding with her family. Germany was occupying the Netherlands, and since Anne Frank and her family were Jewish, they were subject to the Nazi racial laws, like that Jewish people weren't legal citizens and were subject to being forced into concentration camps.

Anne and her family, along with several others, hid in a set of secret rooms concealed by a bookcase above a set of offices. The people who helped conceal them could have faced the death penalty, since protecting people from the Nazi regime was a capital crime.

In August of 1944, two years after they went into

hiding, Anne and her family were discovered and sent to concentration camps. Only her father survived to see the end of the war.

While she was in hiding, Anne kept a detailed diary, which has become a classic. Although she was only in her early teens at the time, Anne's writing was very detailed and powerful, and she dedicated a lot of time to writing and editing her entries. They talk about the war, life in the "secret annex" or hidden rooms, and her thoughts about human nature. One of her most moving quotes was when she wrote, "in spite of everything, I still believe that people are really good at heart… if I look up into the heavens, I think that it will all come right, that this cruelty too will end, and that peace and tranquility will return again."

Elie Wiesel

Another moving memoir of the Holocaust was written by Elie Wiesel, who was born in Romania just a year before Anne was, and who wrote the famous memoir *Night* about his experiences in two concentration camps, Auschwitz and Buchenwald.

While Anne talked in her diary about her faith in the ultimate goodness of humanity, *Night* tells about Wiesel's experience being forced to take care of his helpless father in the concentration camps. Wiesel called *Night* his "deposition," a confession or testimony, because of his feelings of guilt and rage at the horrible things that happened to him. He then went on to write a second two books, titled *Dawn* and *Day*, about experiences of Holocaust survivors (based to varying extents on Wiesel himself but not totally autobiographical) after the war.

Wiesel said of the Holocaust, "Everything came to an end—man, history, literature, religion, God. There was nothing left. And yet we begin again with night," which is how he chose the title of his book. In Judaism, time is measured starting with nightfall, so Wiesel told his story with the idea that World War Two was the night that had to happen before a new day.

Japan's History Textbook Controversy

Germany has gone out of its way in the past half-century to make sure its students are thoroughly educated about World War Two. Students read first-hand accounts like Wiesel's memoir or Frank's diary. It is seen as a very serious topic, and the atrocities of the Nazi army are seriously discussed and understood.

By contrast, the Japanese school textbooks have faced serious controversy for leaving out information about the crimes against humanity that happened early in World War Two. They were accused of leaving out crucial information and "whitewashing" the actions of the Japanese military, especially against China in the 1930s.

The Japanese Society for History Textbook Reform is a conservative "revisionist" group that promotes Japanese nationalism above all other things. In 2005, they wrote their own history textbook, called the *New History Textbook*. Among other things, it summarizes the Nanking Massacre in a footnote by saying:

> At this time, many Chinese soldiers and civilians were killed or wounded by Japanese troops (the Nanking Incident). Documentary evidence has raised doubts about the actual number of victims claimed by the incident.

In case you've forgotten from Chapter One, the estimates about the actual number of victims were between 200,000 and 500,000.

The textbook also says,

> Japanese soldiers drove out the forces of Western Europe, which had colonized the nations of Asia for many years. They surprised us, because we didn't think we could possibly beat the white man, and they inspired us with confidence.

While it's true that European nations had, of course, colonized Asian countries (and treated the colonized countries very badly too), that's not a great reason to be inspired by an army that sided with Hitler and committed thousands of war crimes. There are better role models out there.

How do we Deal with World War Two?

Like it or not, World War Two has changed our world forever. It's inspired great works of literature, including true memoirs and accounts of events by people who actually lived through it (we only got to talk about two of them, but there have been hundreds of memoirs for people involved in every part of the war!). It also changed the world of cinema, since it's now one of the most popular settings for film ever, and has inspired thousands of movies, shows, and documentaries, from all over the world. We wouldn't have the James Bond movies without World War Two. Who would he have worked against in those early days, if not Nazis and Soviets?

Outside of the realm of media, it was World War Two that set the stage for everything that happened in the rest of the twentieth century. It made people want to act in very specific ways, which led to the "era of conformity" of the 1950s, which was then rebelled against in the late '50s, '60s, and '70s by the hippie and peace movements. It also set up the United States and the Soviet Union for the nuclear arms race that would have civilians biting their nails for decades, worrying about "mutually assured destruction."

By learning about World War Two, you will now be able to understand, just a little bit better, why the world is the way it is today!

RANDOM FACTS

1. One of Fritz Lang's 1930s art films, *M*, introduced the idea of marking a degenerate criminal by putting a symbol on his clothes. While Lang was not a fascist, and Hitler actually hated him and his films, the idea of putting a symbol on someone's clothes to mark them as "bad" was one that the Nazis ended up famously using.

2. Charlie Chaplin was on Adolf Hitler's official kill list for his portrayal of Hitler as a bumbling, screaming maniac in the film *The Great Dictator*, Chaplin's first talking role!

3. In *The Great Dictator*, instead of using Hitler's real name, he was called "Adenoid Hynkle." However, while they change the names of many people and groups in the film to similarly "off-brand" versions, the victims in the film are still the Jewish people, and their plight is treated very seriously.

4. Helene "Leni" Riefenstahl was in charge of making Nazi propaganda films, like *Triumph of the Will* and *Olympia*. Her movies have been banned in many places for their hateful content but have also been held up as examples of how propaganda works. She died in 2003 at the age of 101.

5. Although the vast majority of films and books inspired by World War Two have been very serious, there have been a couple of humorous treatments. Two of the most famous are the oddly lighthearted concentration camp story *Life is Beautiful*, and Mel Brooks' comedy classic *The Producers*, which is about two stage producers putting on a show called *Springtime for Hitler*.

6. *Saving Private Ryan* was the highest-grossing World War Two film of all time, at over 216 million dollars... until *Dunkirk* beat it with 462 million.

7. The assault on Dunkirk that was dramatized in Nolan's film *Dunkirk* was halted by Hitler, who believed that his air force could take care of it without the help of the ground soldiers. Not only was he wrong about that, but Nolan doesn't even bring it up in the movie! In fact, Hitler's name is not spoken even once in the entire film.

8. In Germany, World War Two is a huge part of the history curriculum. German students read first-hand accounts from both soldiers and victims, in camps and on the front. It is considered extremely important that children understand history so they don't allow it to happen again. These accounts are known to be very troubling, but they are important to understand.

9. The buildings in Nuremberg that were used by Hitler and the Nazis for rallies are now a museum about the horrors of World War Two.

10. In Canada and England, World War Two is called the Second World War.

11. Anne Frank had plans to turn her diary into a novel after the war. She wanted to call it *The Secret Annex*.

12. No one knows who informed the SS of where Anne Frank and her family were hiding.

13. Anne Frank's diary is one of the most regularly banned books in the world. Some of the reasons are unsurprising—it's an incredibly sad book, written by a child, during the worst war in human history. But another reason is more bizarre. Some people don't like the fact that Anne, like any girl writing in a diary, makes some rather explicit observations about her vagina!

14. In 1986, Elie Wiesel won the Nobel Peace Prize for his works against racial violence and repression.

15. *Night* by Elie Wiesel has been published in over thirty languages (Wiesel himself did both Yiddish and French versions), but although Wiesel has won dozens of awards, the book itself actually hasn't won any. What an oversight!

16. The slogan of the Japanese Society for History

Textbook Reform is "give the children correct history textbooks." It's just that their idea of *correct* is a little questionable.

17. The rest of the world isn't immune from controversy over what makes a "correct" version of World War Two. As with anything in history, there are gaps and things that don't make sense. But that doesn't justify the movement of people who believe the Holocaust was a hoax. Called "Holocaust deniers," they believe that the Nazis only meant to deport, not murder, the Jewish population, and despite both film and written evidence, claim that the death camps were either not real at all or are exaggerated. To be clear: yes, the Holocaust *did* happen.

18. Holocaust denial is actually illegal in Germany, as well as Austria, Hungary, and Romania, which were all Axis powers. It is considered a type of anti-Semitic hate speech, since Holocaust deniers often blame Jewish people for "making up" the Holocaust.

19. It's legal in the United States and the United Kingdom, but if you live in one of those places, you should still try to use your knowledge to educate your friends about why World War Two happened, rather than letting anyone you know get sucked in by deniers!

20. When the next major war broke out after World War Two (the Korean War), Clint Eastwood famously said, "Wait a second, didn't we just get through with that?"

Test Yourself – Questions and Answers

1) Who were the major countries worried about nuclear weapons after World War Two?

   a. The United States and the Soviet Union

   b. Britain and France

   c. Germany and Japan

2) What was the Beat Generation?

   a. The generation of soldiers who were beaten in World War Two

   b. A drumming band that used World War Two marches for inspiration

   c. A group of artists who rebelled against conformity after World War Two

3) Which film was not made by Leni Riefenstahl?

   a. *Triumph of the Will*

   b. *Olympia*

   c. *Metropolis*

4) Which of these movie megastars did Hitler *not* have a problem with?

   a. Charlie Chaplin

   b. Mel Brooks

   c. Fritz Lang

5) Which of these films was the highest-grossing World War Two movie ever?

   a. *Dunkirk*

   b. *Saving Private Ryan*

   c. *Pearl Harbour*

Answers

1. a
2. c
3. c
4. b
5. a

DON'T FORGET YOUR FREE BOOKS

GET THEM FOR FREE ON
WWW.TRIVIABILL.COM

MORE BOOKS BY BILL O'NEILL

I hope you enjoyed this book and learned something new. Please feel free to check out some of my previous books on **Amazon**.

Made in the USA
San Bernardino, CA
12 December 2019

61332618R00098